The
allad of

Gussie & Clyde

The
*B*allad of
Gussie & Clyde

A True Story of True Love

A A R O N L A T H A M

Villard New York

All rights reserved under International and Pan-American Copyright
Conventions. Published in the United States by Villard Books, a
division of Random House, Inc., New York, and simultaneously in
Canada by Random House of Canada Limited, Toronto.

Grateful acknowledgment is made to the following for permission to
reprint previously published material:

HARCOURT BRACE & COMPANY AND FABER AND FABER LIMITED: Three lines
from "Burnt Norton" from *Four Quartets* by T. S. Eliot. Copyright © 1943
by T. S. Eliot. Copyright renewed 1971 by Esme Valerie Eliot. Rights
throughout the world excluding the United States are controlled by Faber
and Faber Limited. Reprinted by permission of Harcourt Brace &
Company and Faber and Faber Limited.

HENRY HOLT & CO., INC. AND JONATHAN CAPE LTD., A DIVISION OF RANDOM
HOUSE U.K.: Six lines from "Reluctance" from *The Poetry of Robert Frost*
edited by Edward Connery Lathem. Copyright © 1923, 1928, 1962
by Robert Frost. Copyright © 1934, 1969 by Henry Holt & Co., Inc.
Rights throughout the British Commonwealth are controlled by Jonathan
Cape Ltd., a division of Random House U.K. Reprinted by permission of
Henry Holt & Co., Inc. and Jonathan Cape Ltd., a division
of Random House U.K.

Villard Books is a registered trademark of Random House, Inc.

Library of Congress Cataloging-in-Publication Data
Latham, Aaron.
The ballad of Gussie and Clyde: a true story of true love/Aaron Latham.
p.   cm.
ISBN 0-679-45675-9 (alk paper)
1. Latham, Clyde.   2. Lancaster, Gussie Lee.   3. Aged—United
States—Biography.   4. Love in old age—United States—Case studies.
I. Title.
HQ1064.U5L375   1997
306.7'084'6—dc21   96-49849

Random House website address:
http://www.randomhouse.com/

Printed in the United States of America on acid-free paper

24689753

TO LESLEY

ALL THE FORESTS ARE ARDEN

AND ALL THE DREAMS MIDSUMMER NIGHTS.

$\mathscr{P}$reface

Old father, old artificer, stand me now and ever in good stead.
  —James Joyce, *A Portrait of the Artist as a Young Man*

In social settings, I am not much of a storyteller. I listen. Occasionally I counterpunch, but I never lead the discussion. Being congenitally shy, I simply can't stand being the focus of attention. So I wasn't pleased one evening at dinner when my wife said:

"You have to tell about your father."

I saw them all staring at me. I was an oyster and they were hungry Walruses and Carpenters inviting me to "come and walk." I was a plate of beans and they were cowboys who had been riding hard all day.

"Well, uh . . ."

I kept expecting somebody else to break in—as so often happens—to tell his or her own story. But for once, nobody else spoke.

"Uh, well, uh, my father's in love . . ."

As I told the story, I noticed something amazing: I

wasn't in pain. My throat didn't close. My mouth wasn't dry. I didn't hate telling this yarn. And I was surprised by something else as well: The Walruses and Carpenters and hungry cowboys were all listening. These were people who had talked to presidents, lunched with Nobel laureates, chatted with stars, even interviewed Steven Spielberg. And they were all leaning forward. None of them had ever met my dad, but they all wanted what he had to give: hope.

Soon I was telling my father's story over and over, at any table I could find, sometimes at my wife's insistence, other times entirely of my own volition. I went from feeling no pain as I told it . . . to liking to tell it . . . to loving the telling.

Then my wife started telling the story, too. She told it better than I did, which was no surprise. Sometimes we told it together. She would start the story, and I would finish it. Or I would open and she would close.

The story kept evolving as we told it, now happier, now sadder, now more poignant . . .

Let me tell you about my father.

The
*B*allad of
Gussie & Clyde

1
Eighty Years Old

"We haven't met for many years," said Daisy.
—F. Scott Fitzgerald, *The Great Gatsby*

It started with my father Clyde's eightieth birthday party, which prompted a family reunion. Brothers and nephews and nieces and cousins came from thousands of miles away to Spur, Texas, a town of 1,300 and shrinking. Spur is in that godforsaken corner of West Texas which is the last stronghold of real cowboys, cattle ranches, rattle-snakes, and tarantula stampedes (at certain times of year). Main Street is just three blocks long and has a single red light that keeps blinking on and off to direct traffic that is no longer there. Some days more tumbleweeds than pickup trucks come rolling through town. The Palace theater's marquee still hangs over Main Street, but its last movie played twenty-five years ago. (It was already out of business when *The Last Picture Show* was filmed on loca-tion in a small town nearby.) Folks wear blue jeans, boots, and even spurs to church on Sunday. And high-school football is bigger than the Super Bowl. My father is a retired West Texas high-school football coach and has always seemed larger-than-life to me.

On the eve of his eightieth birthday, Clyde was still a handsome man. He had real presence, both in stature and in personality. He stood straight at six feet, four inches and weighed about two hundred pounds. And he was charming. I'm afraid I have always been a little intimidated by his charm. He had big, even teeth, and he combed his full head of silver hair straight back. He had high cheekbones and a straight nose that he probably owed to his great-great-grandmother, a Cherokee. The grandson of a Texas Ranger (who fought the Comanches), Clyde spoke with a slight drawl. Age had chiseled his features and slimmed him down, so he looked even better at eighty than he had twenty years ago. "Your father's sexy," my wife says. "He's got tall charm. He's Gary Cooper with a smile and conversation."

Among the relatives and friends who were expected to descend upon Spur to celebrate his eightieth birthday were several women known collectively as the "Willis girls." I had only a vague notion of who these Willises were. They had grown up around Spur but had been gone for a long, long time. They somehow seemed less than kinfolk and more than friends. I wasn't sure why my dad was so happy to hear that they were coming—or so disappointed when they changed their minds. Their excuse was some sort of illness in the family.

Sickness or no sickness, I was mad. How could the Willis girls—now all in their seventies—undermine my father's celebration? How could they back out at the last moment? Didn't they know how much he was looking forward to seeing them again? Yes, I was angry. Angry at a bunch of little old ladies. Old ladies I hardly knew. I certainly didn't know them well enough to get this mad at them. Oh, I had met three of them briefly many years ago; the fourth I had never seen in my life. Still I was as furious as if they were best friends who had double-crossed me.

I simply couldn't stand the thought of my father being disappointed. Never could. When I was growing up, many of my buddies competed with their dads, but I didn't. He was both too big and too gentle to be a rival. When we played canasta and dominoes around my childhood's kitchen table, I always wanted him to win. Later on, I couldn't stand to beat him at golf. Not that I ever had much of a chance. I never came close until he was in his late seventies. But the point is: I didn't want to beat him. And I didn't want anybody else beating him either. Or beating up on him. Those Willis girls had better watch out.

My father had a wonderful eightieth birthday, but there was this one small shadow that fell across his happiness: The Willis girls weren't there.

One of the Willis girls—the one I had never met— saved the invitation.

2
$\mathcal{W}$orld Enough

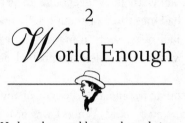

Had we but world enough, and time,
This coyness, lady, were no crime.
　　　　　—Andrew Marvell,
　　　　　　　"To His Coy Mistress"

Just over two years after my father's big party, my mother died. A few days after the funeral, my dad and I played a round of golf on Spur's hardscrabble golf course. On the ninth tee, he surveyed the landscape: scrawny mesquite trees, dying grass, rocks, sand, and a diseased, tick-ridden jackrabbit.

"It's a pretty old world," my father said.

I just stood there shaking my head—because he was right. There was plenty of ugliness in the world, my mother's death at the top of that list, but it was still a pretty old world. Mesquites are not my favorite tree, but it was still a pretty old world. Green grass would have been prettier than brown, but it was still a pretty old world. My dad knew that he had a lot of trials ahead of him, loneliness, a dying body, but it was still a pretty old world. I thought it was one of the bravest, most existential statements I had ever heard. It was courage in the face of tragedy, aesthetics in the face of disaster.

As I later learned, one of the Willis girls lost her husband at about the same time. Her name was Gussie Lee (Willis) Lancaster. In my nightly calls to my dad, I began to hear her name mentioned casually in our conversations. I gathered that Clyde and Gussie talked on the phone from time to time. I was uneasy about this development, since I was still nursing a grudge against Gussie and the other Willis girls.

And of course I felt protective of my father. My dad and I had always been close, but we had become even more so during my mother's final illness. She had been desperately sick in the hospital for six weeks, then home for three weeks but on kidney dialysis, then back in the hospital for a little over three weeks before she died. During all that time, my father had been with her, often twenty-four hours a day. And I had been with the two of them during much of that time. We slept in the same room with her. My father and I ate all our meals together. And we were desperately, hopelessly, miserably sad together. He started to limp. Then he could hardly walk at all. Driving home the day she died, my father lost concentration and ran off the road at seventy miles an hour. We almost flipped. I am convinced that all that saved us was his remembering at the last moment that I was in the car.

After such a shared searing experience—we were wartime comrades, foxhole buddies—I couldn't just walk away from him and call home every week or so as in the past. I was used to talking to him almost every hour of the twenty-four-hour day. The least I could do was call once a day. And of course I worried about him more than I would have if we had not visited hell together. I worried about him being alone so much. But I also worried about his getting hurt. Was Gussie a hurter? So far she hadn't done much else. But I didn't mention my concerns to my father, and those calls to Gussie continued.

These were long calls—geographically and in many other ways—from Spur, Texas, to Sacramento, California. Of course, they talked about—among other things—Spur and how it had changed since Gussie last saw it almost seventy years ago. These discussions would end with Clyde pressing her to return to her old hometown, to see the old buildings, the old movie theater, the old people. She would say maybe someday.

Then my dad would announce: "Well, I have to hang up now."

And *bang* down would go the receiver.

*O*ne evening during our regular call, my father had good news. Or at any rate, he thought it was good.

"Gussie's coming," my dad said, happy as a kid.

She was finally returning to visit the place where she was born and where many of her relatives were buried. Not only had Gussie not seen Spur for nearly seventy years, she hadn't seen Clyde for half a century. My dad was excited.

A couple of days later, he called back with bad news.

"Gussie's not coming," he said, dejected.

"Again," I said.

"Well, somethin' come up."

"I'm sorry."

"I don't know anything."

That was his standard sign-off. I'd heard it thousands of times. But this time it sounded emptier than usual.

"I don't either," I said.

We hung up. I was angry. Pissed off at a little old white-haired lady.

"What's wrong?" asked my wife.

We were in the kitchen of our New York apartment. We live in what amounts to a small house—an afterthought—built on top of a fifteen-story building. We overlook the Museum of Natural History on the West Side of Manhattan.

"Gussie," I said angrily. "She's not coming."

"Aaron, you can't be mad at a little old lady you don't even know," my wife said.

"Why not?"

"Grow up. Does your dad know how you feel?"

"No, I don't want to make him feel even worse."

"Good."

"But I hope he's learned his lesson. I hope he doesn't ask her to come down again."

"Don't say that. You're always so worried about him being alone. *You* know that being alone too much isn't good for you."

She paused to glare at me. As a writer, I did know a lot about loneliness. It is an occupational hazard that can sap your energy and your optimism—or worse. And I was indeed concerned about my father's isolation since my mother's death.

"You should be glad," Lesley continued, "that he's reaching out to somebody."

"I would be if the reaching did any good," I said, "but this isn't ever going to work. The only thing worse than being alone is being alone and pining for somebody."

*S*everal months later, the homecoming trip was back on. My dad sounded energetic. He was making plans for showing Gussie around. Then she backed out again, and his disappointment was audible.

I was angrier than ever. Gussie had hurt my father again. I couldn't stand it. I remembered so many other hurts. When I was very young, he almost died after an operation to remove bone spurs from his heels. The coach wanted to run with his players—to show them how instead of telling them how—so he had gone in for what should have been minor surgery. A Fort Worth doctor botched it. My dad's eyes rolled up, and he stopped breathing. He saw himself slipping down a long slide into black water. Everything went black and stayed black . . .

Then he came back to life.

But the circulation in his legs would continue to be a problem for the rest of his life. They swelled, peeled, turned black. Then they got better. Then worse. I remember lying in bed, early in the morning or late at night, listening to my dad's distinctive footsteps, trying to hear how his legs were doing. Was today a good day or a bad day? How was he feeling? Would he get sick again and really die this time? Could he go down into the black water and never come up? My father was so big and strong—he looked so healthy—and yet he was so vulnerable. Didn't this Willis girl understand? He didn't need any more hurts.

3

$\mathcal{T}$hanksgiving

> Where the city of the healthiest fathers stands,
> Where the city of the best-bodied mothers stands,
> There the great city stands.
> —Walt Whitman, "Song of the Broad-Axe"

I was having trouble with the movies. I had had a wonderful experience with the first film I wrote, *Urban Cowboy*, which was about a mechanical bull; a less wonderful time with my second, *Perfect*, about a health club; and a horrific bout with my third, *The Program*, about a college football team. Of course, I had originally been attracted to the project because my father had been a football coach.

The horror began when I got a call from a reporter at *Newsday* who told me that some teenagers had tried to duplicate a stunt in the movie with tragic results. They had gone out in the middle of a highway, lain down on their backs on the dotted yellow line, and played traffic roulette with their lives. At least one had been killed. I was shaken.

At first, I felt guilty, painfully guilty, but then I began to think of extenuating circumstances. In the movie, we had presented the stunt as a dangerous, irresponsible act. Moreover, I hadn't made up this scene out of pure imagination. I had spent two seasons thoroughly researching college football. I ate dinner every night with the players at Penn State. I worked out with the team at the University of Virginia. And I served as honorary assistant coach at the University of Southern California, where my chief duty was to tell three-hundred-pounders to turn out the lights and go to sleep at 10 P.M. I was always amazed that they obeyed me.

While I was living with these football teams, I heard stories of players taking part in many dangerous stunts. One was lying down in the middle of a highway and daring cars and trucks to do their worst. So these road games were happening before we made our movie. Consequently, it was unclear whether these most recent stunts were a continuation of something begun in the past—or whether we had inspired them. No one was even sure whether the unfortunate daredevil teens had even seen *The Program*.

Besides, weren't people, even teenage boys, responsible for their own actions? Am I ranting yet?

When I first heard that the Walt Disney Studio might recall the movie and cut the highway scene, I wasn't really against it. But then I had second thoughts. By the time Disney did cut the scene, I had come to the conclusion that it was a mistake. It was a bad precedent.

I exonerated myself and the movie. But then I relapsed into guilt, albeit of a paler shade. Then I made another impassioned plea to that jury in my head and managed to convince myself: Not guilty! Then guilty again, then not, then . . .

I was having a bad time.

Then everything got a lot worse. Late one autumn night, my wife, Lesley, told me that she thought we should separate. She asked me to move out but to live nearby so I could continue to see our daughter, Taylor, regularly. I was startled and devastated. I told her how surprised I was. She said my surprise was proof that I had become totally withdrawn and uncommunicative.

I said I had been having a hard time.

Although it was late, I got up and went out. As Hemingway wrote of the aftermath of a bad moment with his wife: "I remember what I did in the night."

Maybe I would go to Spur and live with my father for a while.

A couple of days later, still living at home out of stubborn inertia, I lay on my "work" couch staring at the ceiling. I should have been sitting at my nearby desk really working, but I wasn't. I told myself that maybe I would find an idea up there on the tabula rasa suspended above my head, even though I never had before. Well, rarely anyway. The telephone rang. I thought about not answering. I suspected that any news was bound to be bad news, and I didn't need any more.

"Hello," I said in a low voice.

"Hello, how are you?"

I was disappointed to hear the voice of my wife calling from work. I was right. I shouldn't have answered. I was pretty sure she hadn't phoned to make me feel better.

"Not too good," I said.

"I'm sorry," she said. "I've been thinking. Maybe we should put what I said on hold. See what happens."

"Really?"

"Let's just see."

"All right. Good."

"Good."

As I was saying, I was glad I answered the phone.

A week or so later, Lesley surprised me again. We were sitting in the living room looking out at the roof of the Museum of Natural History. I felt formal and uneasy. I didn't want to be uncommunicative, but at the same time I was afraid of saying the wrong thing.

"I've been thinking," said Lesley. "Your father's all alone. Maybe we should invite him to come up for Thanksgiving."

I thought: She is telling me, without saying it, of course, that we are still a family. And families should be together on important holidays. I was thankful for this Thanksgiving offering.

"That's a good idea," I said. "I'll ask him. Thanks."

"Maybe he'll come here for a couple of days first," she said. "Then we'll take him up to Swampscott for the big day. What do you think?"

"Good."

This invitation was not only welcome, not only a surprise, but it was actually unprecedented. Almost historic. For my father had never met my wife's mother or father. We had eloped, so they hadn't met at our wedding. When Taylor was born, my dad pulled into town just as Lesley's parents were pulling out. They barely missed each other.

My mother was another story. For some reason, now forgotten, my mom arrived to see her first and only grandchild a couple of days before my dad was able to get away. Launa (Lay-YOU-nah) Latham met Dolly and Lou Stahl in the George Washington University Hospital room where the brand-new mother was recovering from a cesarean section. My mother was on one side of the bed, Lesley's on the other.

Dolly started unpacking a box of Baby Dior fashions for infants. The clothes really were handsome, but Lesley was too exhausted and druggy to notice. Her eyelids were descending. Dolly felt unappreciated, but she didn't want to criticize her "baby," the new mother, who was failing to ooh and aah. Sadly she looked around the room and then locked on my mother.

"Come on, Mrs. Latham," the other grandmother said, "try to show a little more enthusiasm!"

We all laughed—even, after a moment, Dolly and my mother.

When my father finally arrived, he showed plenty of enthusiasm for his new granddaughter, Taylor. I still have a vivid memory of his holding her in just one hand. She was so small and he was so big: She just fit. Like a clam on the half shell, a bird on its nest, a cup on its saucer, soup in its bowl.

My father's heart was big, too, literally. His doctors had told him years ago that he had an enlarged heart and that it beat irregularly, like Taylor's during her last few dangerous minutes in the womb. The syncopated heart. And now that huge heart, like that huge hand, held his granddaughter, who would grow up to look like—and in many ways *be* like—the daughter he had lost, killed on the highway, when she was just twenty-one years old. Taylor couldn't heal that wound, but she would dull the pain. Staring down at her in the palm of his hand, did he already sense what she would become? Was the hurt already ebbing? He certainly did look happy to make her acquaintance. I was so glad she was a daughter.

As Taylor grew up, Lesley and I never made any special efforts to bring together her two sets of grandparents. They lived so far apart, my folks out west, my wife's in Swampscott north of Boston; Lesley's parents inhabiting a mansion at the very edge of the Atlantic Ocean, mine holed up in a middle-class house on a decaying, land-locked street. We simply didn't think Dolly & Lou and Clyde & Launa could possibly have much in common, and so we left them at what seemed opposite sides of the world.

I called my father, as I did every day, but this time with a new urgency.

"I need your help with something," I said. "We would like to invite you to come up for Thanksgiving. Lesley suggested it. You know we've been having problems lately. I think a real family Thanksgiving might help."

"Sure."

"You're up to it?"

"Of course."

"You're feeling all right?"

"Fine."

*W*hen my tall father walked into the mansion by the sea, entering a living room that was almost as big as his home, all the women in the house started to "twitter." The word was Lesley's, not mine. The formidable Dolly started to flirt with him. One of Dolly's oldest friends, Clarita, insisted on showing him the grounds. Younger women were interested, too. I had never had such a reception in this house or any other. In many ways, I am not my father's son. (Well, maybe I was just feeling a little insecure because my wife had recently wanted to throw me out of my home.)

Clyde might be in his eighties, but he was nonetheless something new, something fresh, a Marlboro Man who had charm instead of sissy cigarettes. With his high cheekbones and proud nose, he might have been the original Indian come to Thanksgiving in Massachusetts.

Clyde stared at the huge—large as a 70-mm movie screen—window that framed a classic view of the ocean breaking on jagged rocks. It was a Winslow Homer canvas, a page out of Melville.

"It's a pretty old world," my father said, with the same intonation he had used when staring out at the ragged Spur golf course with its mangy jackrabbits.

"It is pretty," said Dolly.

Not only did Clyde excite the women of the house, he also got on well with Lesley's father. More than well. When we got up the next morning, we found the two of them, Clyde and Lou, having coffee together in the kitchen. They had been up since five o'clock, talking, sipping. The rest of the day, they were inseparable. The women were jealous.

And we had thought they wouldn't have anything in common. They had us in common, of course. Somehow we had missed that. And they had their generation in common. Clyde had already passed the eighty benchmark, and Lou would soon. Together they remembered what fewer and fewer did. They shared a knowledge of what it felt like to grow old. Not have anything in common? They couldn't get enough of each other.

What a mistake we had made. Bringing up dads is tricky.

Fifteen-year-old Taylor made the turkey. She just loved to cook. Unlike her mother, Lesley. Unlike her grandmother Launa. Unlike me. But exactly like my sister, Sharon. They even loved to cook the same things: turkeys, brownies, Rice Krispie treats. . . . If I believed in second comings . . . but unfortunately I don't.

We had a wonderful Thanksgiving. My father helped patch up my marriage. And maybe cost himself a roommate.

4
Almost

But bowed his comely head
Down, as upon a bed.
—Andrew Marvell,
"An Horation Ode upon
Cromwell's Return from Ireland"

As soon as my father got back to Spur, he started calling Gussie again. The old pattern repeated itself over and over, month in, month out: Gussie was coming. No she wasn't. Yes she was. No. Yes. Sorry.

I had long since figured out that she was never coming. But my dad continued to brighten with each promise and fade with each change of plans.

I kept getting madder.

Then in October—the month my mother had died—Gussie (Willis) Lancaster again agreed to come down to see her old hometown. Her daughter, Nola, would accompany her on the trip.

"She's really coming this time," my father assured me.

"Really?" I said.

This time the plans actually did seem more definite, but I still wasn't fooled.

When my dad phoned me on the morning of October 6th—the day Gussie was supposed to fly—I knew what to expect.

"Gussie just called," my father said.

"Oh, no," I said.

"She may not be able to come after all."

"What a surprise!"

How could she keep doing this to him? Was she some kind of octogenarian tease? Who needed her? I actually found myself saying to myself: My mother would never have treated my father this way.

"Somethin' come up."

"Again."

"Well—"

"You shouldn't get your hopes up."

It was the same old story. I hated this woman. Why couldn't my father see what she was really like? Why did he persist? Why did he keep inviting blow after blow? Did he enjoy being wounded? Was that the answer? Was that why he had been hurt so often?

"He can't stand this," I told my wife. "He really can't."

We were in our upstairs bedroom. It was small, but we could see for miles.

"Are you sure it's not you who can't stand it?" Lesley asked.

"Well, I can't stand it either. I'm really worried about him."

"You're so protective of him. It's like you're the parent, and he's the kid with a crush."

"Mom died today."

"Oh." My wife paused. "Yes, of course."

"Two years ago exactly."

I was afraid that another disappointment on top of that sad memory might be almost too much for my father.

*L*ater that day, the phone rang again.

"She's got as far as Dallas," my father said.

"Really?"

I couldn't believe it. Had I misjudged this woman? I certainly hoped so. Maybe my father was a better judge of character than I was, after all. He certainly sounded happy, and I was glad for him. We said good-bye to each other and I sat there wondering what would happen next.

The phone rang again. I knew what was coming.

"Don't tell me," I said. "She's not coming."

"There's some kinda problem with the flight from Dallas to Lubbock," my father said. "She's talkin' about turnin' around and goin' right back home."

The problem was that there was room for one of them on the plane—mother or daughter—but not both. Gussie didn't think she could make the trip without Nola. She was a nervous traveler anyway, and she had no idea what might be waiting for her in Spur. Gussie just couldn't face such an ordeal alone. Sorry. It was just too much to ask and more than she could do.

"I warned you not to get your hopes up," I reminded him.

But this news didn't seem to cheer him up. Poor man, Tantalus Agonistes.

5

𝒫roblems

"Captain Wentworth is not very gallant by you, Anne. . . .
He said: 'You were so altered he should not have known
you again.'"

—Jane Austen, *Persuasion*

Around 2:30 that afternoon, Gussie called from Dallas
once again. She told Clyde she was attempting to work up
the nerve to fly halfway across Texas by herself. She wasn't
sure she could do it, but—

"I'll try," she said.

"I'm leaving for the airport right now," he said. "I'll be
there when you step off the plane."

"Wait—"

Gussie warned that she might not be on the plane, but
if she was, she would be wearing a black two-piece suit
and a red blouse. Clyde didn't pay much attention because
he was sure he would know her. Nor did he mention what
he would be wearing. He was in too big a hurry.

My father got into his old Ford—a maroon Crown Victoria—and headed for the nearest airport, which was seventy miles away, in Lubbock. He was getting his hopes up again. More than ever this time.

*T*hat afternoon around five o'clock, Clyde Latham met a Dallas-Lubbock flight and studied the passengers getting off. His disappointment grew. She wasn't on the plane. She hadn't come. She was never coming. His unfocused eyes stared off into the distance, so he didn't see a woman in a black suit and red blouse studying him.

Gussie was upset that Clyde didn't recognize her. She had had no trouble recognizing him because he was the tallest person in the airport. She felt an impulse to turn around and go home to Sacramento. And yet she couldn't help noticing that Clyde—who was wearing tan pants, tan shoes, and a fire-engine red baseball cap that said "Disney Studio"—still looked good.

Gussie marched right up to him and demanded: "Are you Clyde Latham?"

Startled and pleased, suddenly smiling, he admitted: "Why, yes, I am."

They headed for baggage claim. Realizing he had gotten off to a bad start, my father was determined to try to make amends. Was the Clyde charm up to this test?

"I'm sorry I didn't recognize you right off," he said.

"I know why," Gussie said. "You weren't looking for a little old lady."

"No, that's not it. I *was* looking for a little old lady. That was the problem. When no little old ladies got off the plane, I was stumped."

"Liar."

"Cross my old heart."

"Sure." She was still mad. "If you say so."

They went to get her luggage from baggage claim. Clyde hadn't recognized Gussie before, but now he was beginning to. He saw in her hints of the teenager and later the young woman whom he had known. She had been a real beauty in her youth, and she was still a very good-looking woman. He could see that. Anybody could. She still had an age-defying, Coke-bottle figure, and her face was still an attractive oval. Yes, it was a pretty old world.

Gussie was thinking about the strange shape of the fields she had seen from the air. They were round, one round field after another. Inside the circle, the earth was green, outside all was brown. It seemed an unearthly landscape. The circles reminded her of craters on the moon. What strange land was she about to explore? And yet this land had once been her home, and this man once her friend. How everything had changed—including her, so changed that her old friend didn't even recognize her.

Gussie did recognize her single bag, which they collected, and then they headed for the car. She had deliberately packed for only four days, so she would have an excuse for a short visit. When her clothes ran out, she would have to go home. Today was Thursday, so she would have to leave by Monday at the latest. Otherwise she would have to do the unthinkable: wear the same clothes twice in the same week. Now she was gladder than ever that she had had the foresight to arrange an unbreakable excuse for decamping soon. She had no intention of getting stuck in a very small town with this big man who hadn't even known her.

"Welcome home," Clyde said.

"I never planned to come back here," Gussie said.

It was certainly an uncertain start, but my father was up to the challenge. It was a measure of his charm that by the time they drove out of the airport parking lot they were holding hands.

6
A Live-In

Listen for dear honor's sake,
Goddess of the silver lake.
—John Milton, *Comus*

Clyde could have shown a senior citizen's card and paid only eighty-eight cents to the parking-lot attendant, but now didn't seem the time. He paid three dollars and hit the road for the seventy-mile drive home.

"Did you eat on the plane?" asked my father.

"No, I just took Di-Gel pills," Gussie said. "I had a terrible pain in my stomach. But now I'm hungry."

Her son-in-law was a pilot for American, but she still hated flying.

"We'll stop at the lake on the way home."

Going home, Clyde had to decide between Highway 82, which ran through a series of small towns, and Route 40, which ran through farm after farm. The towns on 82 were all about twelve miles apart because back in Wild West days that was how often stagecoaches needed to change

horses. But since Clyde wanted to be alone with Gussie—
and show her the country, which was much more impressive than the towns—he picked Route 40. It was the first
of many long drives down narrow roads. Gussie was feeling proud of herself for having been brave enough to make
this trip after so many years.

She was surprised at how easy Clyde was to talk to, and
he felt the same way. At first, they talked about their families. Gussie's daughter, Nola, was married to Tom Hall,
the pilot. They had a married daughter, Annie, and another daughter, Colleen, whose dream was to attend the
Air Force Academy on her way to becoming a Top Gun jet
fighter pilot. Like dad, like daughter. Gussie also had a
son, Fred, who was an advertising man in northern California. He was married to Dorothy, an IBM executive.

Clyde also had two children, but one of them, Sharon,
had been killed by drag racers. He didn't like to talk about
that. His son, Aaron, a writer, lived in New York City,
which he loved because it was big, like Texas. He was
married to 60 Minutes correspondent Lesley Stahl. Their
daughter, Taylor, planned to direct movies when she grew
up—or even before.

"How can you stand being around somebody so fa-
mous?" Gussie asked.

"You mean Lesley?" Clyde said. "It's easy."

Eventually he got around to explaining the round fields.
They were created by an irrigation system that resembled
the hands on a clock. The well was at the center of the
clock. The hands were sprinklers that moved around the
face of the clock on wheels. To Gussie the landscape
started feeling less strange, less foreign.

"Look at that cotton," she said.

She was impressed with the farms. Gussie hadn't seen such an abundance of cotton fields in almost seventy years. She hadn't exactly missed them, since she hated picking cotton as a girl, but now they stirred some tender emotion. She noticed that the cotton stalks were so much bigger than they had been when she was young. Usually when you go home again, everything looks smaller because you are bigger, but not this time. Scientists had been busy creating bigger plants while she was away. And these new hybrids were covered with many more cotton bolls than when last they met.

But Gussie missed something.

"What happened to all the houses?" she asked. "Where are all the people?"

"They just dried up and blew away," Clyde said, "like a buncha old tumbleweeds."

While the cotton had gotten bigger, the number of farmhouses had grown smaller. When Gussie was a girl, there were houses every few fields. The land might support more cotton now, but in the old days it had supported more folks. Now many of the small farmers had been driven out of business. Bigger farms had swallowed the smaller ones. The few prosperous farmers then moved to town and commuted to work on their farms.

After driving for forty miles across a vast pool table— the cotton was the green felt—they came to the ragged edge of the Great Plains. Here the caprock—the giant stone floor that keeps the plains flat—had eroded away. The car rolled off the great flatness and down into broken country. The rectangular farms gave way to rugged ranch land. Canyons. Hills. Breaks. Ravines. Exposed red earth. And, of course, mesquite trees. Lots of mesquites.

"Look at all the mesquite trees," Gussie said, new energy in her voice. "Aren't they pretty?"

They were considerably bigger and more numerous than they had been long ago.

"The ranchers hate them things," Clyde said. "They crowd out the grass."

"I don't care. I love them."

"Free country."

"I remember on hot days, runnin' between Granny's place and yours. Barefoot. My feet always blistered. The only shade was under those mesquite trees that your ranchers hate."

After driving and talking for sixty miles, Gussie saw something else that hadn't been there seventy years ago: water. During the time she had been away, a dam had been built across a stream known as White River to form a lake. Gussie associated this part of the country with droughts. There had never been enough water for the cotton or for anything else. Now here was this West Texas oasis, White River Lake. This once familiar setting was so changed that it hardly seemed real. She felt she had entered some sort of fairy-tale landscape. It was dusk, and lights reflected in the abundant water. The beauty caught Gussie off guard.

Something else caught her off guard too: laughter. She felt that she had been crying for two years, ever since her Bill died, and now she was laughing. It was water to a parched soul. Lights were coming back on inside.

My father, the storyteller, was in good form: "One time,

I poured sorghum syrup in Dad's bedroll. Boy howdy, was he ever sticky and was he ever mad!"

Gussie laughed and laughed.

"He never could figure which one of us did it," Clyde continued, "so he was gonna whup us all, but Mom wouldn't let him."

Gussie laughed some more.

"Did I ever tell you about the Great Goat Drive?" Clyde asked.

"I don't think so," laughed Gussie.

"Well, Uncle Charley had this big herd of goats. He run them on the old Oh Bar Ranch. You know, the letter O with a line under it." Like so O.

"Oh!" said Gussie with a smile.

"His lease run out down there and they talked him into bringin' those goats to Carlsbad. He drove them out there like cattle. Just like an old-time cattle drive. They got out there and he sold them to Old Man Demoss. He wore a gun all the time, a six-gun, strapped to his leg. One time he'd gotten in a gunfight, got his right thumb shot off. They say you're supposed to thumb back the hammer of a six-gun, but he didn't have a thumb."

"A goat drive?" Gussie said, laughing. "Well, that must've been about the last nail in the coffin of the Old West."

"I expect so."

They stopped at the Cattleman's Restaurant—a rather unusual name for an eatery perched on the bank of a lake, with great views of shimmering water—but then this was West Texas. Getting out of the car, Gussie felt the wind pulling at her black skirt and white hair. She had forgotten about the wind, but now she remembered. The wind always seemed to blow in this part of Texas. It started somewhere up in Canada and blew down across the Great Plains—where there was nothing to get in its way—and then spilled down off the caprock. It had come thousands of miles to mess up her hairdo and to whip up whitecaps on the surface of the lake.

"One day the wind stopped blowing," Clyde said, "and all the chickens fell over."

Gussie was glad to get inside, out of the wind. She and Clyde were the only ones in the restaurant, which seemed to have been built just for them. It was the essence of romance. They were on a date. It felt strange but good. Gussie and Clyde both ate fried catfish, which were twisted and gnarled like arthritic fingers.

After dinner, they drove on into town and stopped at the Methodist preacher's parsonage. Clyde had more or less adopted the minister and his wife ever since they arrived in town. Actually even before they got there. On his first Mother's Day without my mom, my dad had gotten restless, climbed into his old Ford, and headed for Abilene, some 150 miles away. He went to look at and listen to Spur's new minister, who was preaching a last sermon in his old church before moving to his new one. Clyde liked the minister and told him so after the service. They soon became close friends.

Clyde parked his old maroon Ford in front of the preacher's house, which is located in one of the tonier parts of Spur—if that isn't an oxymoron. Clyde hadn't called beforehand. He just dropped in. This was Spur.

Clyde was delighted to introduce Gussie Lee Willis

Lancaster to Jack and Ellen Moffatt. The preacher looked like a truck driver, his wife like a teacher. After the handshakes, Ellen asked where Gussie would be staying. The preacher's wife knew there weren't any hotels in Spur, not exactly a tourist Mecca.

"At my house," Clyde said.

"Ah!" exclaimed the preacher's wife. "A live-in!"

Everybody laughed. It was not only funny, it was also good gossip. Gussie knew that by morning everybody in town would know where she was staying and what the preacher's wife had said. She had a moment of uncertainty. She didn't want to be talked over. But then her courage mounted as she reminded herself: She was only going to be in Spur for a short time; then she would go home and would never see these gossips again for the rest of her life. So what did she care what they said?

7

$\mathcal{A}$unt Minnie

Got shot in the breast, I am dying today.
—"The Streets of Laredo"

"Don't worry about the town gossips," Clyde said as they headed toward his house and their first night under the same roof. "They're immaterial to me. The Lathams woulda been run outa Texas a long time ago if we cared about gossips. Did I ever tell you about my Aunt Minnie?"

"Clyde, I haven't talked to you for fifty years," Gussie said. "I don't know any of your stories."

"Good. Well, Aunt Minnie was my aunt on my father's side . . ."

She was a black-haired, dark-eyed beauty with high Cherokee cheekbones. She met Uncle Will, married, and set up housekeeping in the still-wild cowtown of Snyder.

Her beauty got her in trouble, for Aunt Minnie was pursued by a prominent Snyder businessman. Eventually she succumbed to his charm and position. The affair was so much gossiped about that even Uncle Will finally heard.

When he confronted his wife—telling her he knew that she had been unfaithful—she said she could prove she didn't love her supposed lover.

"How?" asked Uncle Will.

"Watch," said Aunt Minnie.

She dressed all in black and went downtown. Seeing her lover across the street, she motioned him over. He hurried across to meet her, smiling.

When he got close enough, Aunt Minnie pulled out a silver six-gun and shot him dead. No love. Proof positive. Q.E.D.

"No, Aunt Minnie never spent a day in jail," Clyde told Gussie. "Folks figured it was all right for a married woman to shoot her lover if'n it saved her marriage. Besides, a lotta money changed hands."

Some fifty years later, Aunt Minnie beat Uncle Will to death with a broom handle. Times had changed. The broom had replaced the pistol, but love remained a deadly game in Texas. No, Aunt Minnie didn't go to jail that time either. Maybe they thought she was justified after a half century of housekeeping and housecleaning for Uncle Will.

And that wasn't the only scandal. One was considerably closer to home. In this case, a particular home, Granny's home, where they would be going tomorrow.

When Clyde and Gussie got "home," my father called to say that she had actually made it to Spur, as promised, this time. Right away, I started worrying about what would happen to him—how would he feel?—when she went back to California. Maybe it would have been better if she had never come at all.

8
ℱleas!

Wherein could this flea guilty be,
Except in that drop which it sucked from thee?
—John Donne, "The Flea"

Gussie is a very ladylike lady. She gets up every morning and gets dressed to go out whether she is going out or not. Not only does she never wear the same outfit twice in the same week, she rarely does in the same month. She is uptown and was understandably worried that she might not be able to cope with small town. And she soon realized that she certainly couldn't cope with something else as well: fleas! Gussie and fleas! They went together like *Sonnets from the Portuguese* and limericks based on Nantucket.

That first night, Thursday night, Gussie slept in the spare bedroom at the back of the house. Unfortunately, it happened to be a room where Clyde's two dogs—Star and Boots—liked to play and nap. Actually, they were originally my mother's dogs and may have been loyally defending her turf by scattering fleas. All night poor Gussie rolled and tossed in her borrowed bed, living a real dog's life.

The next morning, Friday, she announced that she was leaving that bedroom . . . leaving the house . . . leaving Spur . . . leaving Texas and never coming back. She wouldn't spend another night in a house with fleas!

"Take me to the airport," she demanded.

Clyde responded by calling several exterminators and unleashing them on his home. Then he persuaded Gussie to stay at least one more day and night. He promised that by bedtime all the fleas would be as dead as the Dalton Gang, or something to that effect.

With one crisis defused—at least for another few hours—Clyde took Gussie on a sightseeing tour. Some people might have trouble believing that Spur had sights worth seeing, but Clyde had taken time and worked out an itinerary that he hoped would appeal to his special guest.

Gussie was dressed in the first of the four—and only four—outfits she had packed. A black-and-white pantsuit with a paisley vest. Clyde approved.

They started with a drive down Spur's Main Street. Gussie saw a boulevard dominated by a tall, thin sign that stuck right up into the big West Texas sky. White letters were stacked one on top of the other spelling out:

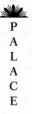

P
A
L
A
C
E

Just above the P was a design that looked like a sunrise, but of course the sun had set on this movie palace years ago. This skinny sign suggested a drum major's baton, and once Main Street had been a kind of parade, especially on weekends, but this parade had long since passed the little town by. The red-brick buildings on both sides of the theater were empty also. Their windows had been bricked up, giving the impression of eyes sewn shut. The Cadillac sign still hung over the sidewalk, but the cars had long since gotten away. There weren't any cars on the street either.

Clyde and Gussie passed a park that had once been a hospital.

"That's where Aaron was born," he said.

𝒥t had been a difficult birth. My big head was too large for my mother's small pelvis. After several days of struggle, the doctor finally decided to remove me in pieces by forceps in order to try to save my mother's life. Fortunately, I had a very mushy head: Instead of a single soft spot on top, I had a huge one. I was an over-ripe melon with hardly any skullbone at all. My head formed itself into a cone and made the hazardous journey in one piece. Being soft-headed saved my life. When my father saw me in the delivery room, he was appalled: His son was a living dunce cap. He rushed out of the hospital. When he returned several hours later, my dad was stunned: His son was no longer a sharpened pencil.

"What a beautiful head!" my father exclaimed.

"What?" asked my mom. "What's so special about his head?"

"Look at it! It's gorgeous!"

"Clyde, don't let fatherhood go to your head."

Later, when my mother learned of the doctor's plan of birth on the installment plan, one piece at a time, she was furious.

"I had to sell a cow to pay for Aaron," my father told Gussie.

*C*lyde and Gussie headed out into the country. They drove on a dirt road between cotton fields, followed by a long plume of dust. The bolls were open and looked like millions of dirty snowballs. Gussie and Clyde held hands as they drove through the countryside. The wind was blowing hard, and the air smelled faintly of alkali.

"Stop!" said Gussie.

Clyde slammed on the brakes, and the car skidded.

"What's wrong?" he asked.

"Nothing. I just want to pick some cotton."

"Pick cotton? Now that you're home again, you just can't wait to turn back into a cotton picker?"

"I hated it when I was a kid, but it's different now. The cotton's different. The stalks're so tall, and the bolls're so big and white and fluffy. I'd love to pick this cotton."

Clyde pulled over to the side of the road and stopped. Gussie hopped out and plunged into the cotton. She bent over and started picking. The great wads of cotton came out of the husks so easily. When she was a girl, the wads had been smaller and tighter. Those had been hard to pull, and the husks had cut her child's hands. But picking this new cotton was actually fun. She hurried back to the car with her arms full of white fluff.

Getting back in the car, Gussie buried her nose in her fresh-picked cotton. She knew how good it would smell, so white and clean, just like a freshly ironed blouse. She rooted around in the fluff like a pig sniffing out truffles.

Achew! Achew! Acheeewwwww!

Gussie couldn't stop sneezing. Gasping and sneezing. Choking. Tears rolled down her cheeks. She grabbed Clyde's arm and hung on tight as if she were drowning.

"I'm going to heave!" she sobbed. "I'm really going to heave!"

"I guess I should've warned you," Clyde said, sniffing the cotton without getting too close. "Only I never thought of it. Really it never occurred to me it would smell so—"

"Worse than a skunk!"

Clyde went on to explain that modern farmers sprayed the cotton with chemicals that made all the leaves dry up and fall off. With the leaves gone, they could pick the cotton with machines instead of by hand. Little girls no longer broke their backs or hurt their hands in West Texas cotton fields. But the chemicals smelled—

"Really worse than a skunk!"

Gussie threw the cotton out the window and they drove on.

"Stop."

"You're not gonna pick cotton again, are you?"

"No, just stop."

Gussie got out and rubbed her hands in the dirt to try to clean the smell off them. She probably hadn't had her fingers in dirt for half a century. She was too much a lady to dirty her hands. But now all that didn't matter. She just wanted to get that smell off of her, and she didn't care how. She shook her hands, clapped them together, and then got back in the car.

They were headed south to see Red Hill—so called because it is made of red clay—where they had both grown up on neighboring farms. The landscape grew damper.

"Looks like it's been rainin' out here," Clyde said.

There didn't seem to have been any rain at all when Gussie was a girl, but now the road was muddy. Clyde's car struggled through the red-mud ruts. Years ago on such a road, his car had skidded into a ditch, but not to worry; he got out, picked it up, and set it back on the road. Of course, he only lifted one end at a time. Now he knew very well he couldn't pull off such a stunt, so he hoped he wouldn't get stuck.

"Did I ever tell you about our burro named Dynamite?" Clyde asked.

"No, I don't think so," said Gussie.

"Well, Pop bought him and brought him home." Pop, that was what the six Latham boys—Glen, Joe, Clyde, Abo, John, and Francis—called their father. "Pop and Abo got up on him. That burro took three steps and fell over dead."

They were on their way to pay a visit to the homesite where Clyde had been born on August 30, 1910. He was pretty sure that Gussie would want to see it because she had been born there, too, three years later on June 30, 1913. This double history was more than a mere coincidence. There was a story behind it, but it wasn't a story the family told very often—if ever. Never to me . . .

Of course, when they reached this place where they had both been born—three years apart but under the same roof—the house was gone, roof and all. It was a casualty of the displacement of small farmhouses by bigger houses in town.

"There's nothing there," Gussie said. "Nothing left at all."

"I told you there wouldn't be," Clyde reminded her.

Gussie's eyes glistened as she stared at what wasn't there anymore. Gussie is a crier.

"It doesn't even look like it," she said. "Are you sure this is the right place?"

"Well, there's seventy years of mesquites out there," Clyde said. "Yeah, I'm sure. This is it." He laughed. "One time my dad and I were out riding, me in front, him in back. And I asked him, 'Pop, how many mesquite trees are there in the world?' He just shook his head. Well, however many there were then, there're about seventy times as many now."

There was nothing to see but thorny mesquite trees and careless weeds, but it was still a pretty old world.

9
$\mathcal{P}$ink Ice Cream

Honor thy father and thy mother.
—Exodus 20:12

While my father was driving Gussie around the country in his Crown Victoria, I was driving my desk. I was trying to write a screenplay, tapping sporadically on my notebook computer, but preoccupied. Like a driver constantly shifting his gaze from road to scenery, I kept moving my attention from my keyboard to my daydreams of the past. My dad was out on a date, and I was remembering my mother—the mother who had made me a writer.

My mother's pioneer ancestors crossed the Mississippi shortly after the Civil War. They crowded all their belongings onto a ferry and set off to conquer the river. Besides plows, furniture, and pots and pans, they were surrounded by chickens, ducks, pigs, and cattle. In the middle of the Mississippi, the cows got upset and started kicking each other. A valuable longhorn milk cow was booted overboard and was in danger of being swept down the river and drowned. One of the boys reached out, grabbed hold of one long horn, and held on all the way across the wide Mississippi. He saved the cow and milk for the family.

They settled for a time in Missouri and then moved on to Texas in a covered wagon. They entered a sea of wild grass that rippled in amber waves. The grass was stirrup high and there weren't any mesquite trees. It was still the golden-grass age on the High Plains.

In those days, the few settlers in the Texas Panhandle lived in dugouts. These homes were half underground, half above, with walls and even roofs made of sod. The pioneers lived this way because they were convinced that the constant high winds would blow over an above-ground house made of wood. My great-grandfather decided to challenge the winds. He imported milled planks and started construction on a home—on top of the ground. His far-flung neighbors dropped by to make fun of him the way Noah's had.

The constant wind huffed and puffed but couldn't blow the plank house down. Soon everybody was building wooden homes on the plains.

$\mathcal{I}$'m sure I became a writer because my mother wanted to be a writer. I am a member of that generation who lived out their mothers' dreams because back then women were not encouraged to pursue their own. She became a teacher because that was the best job open to women in those days.

My mom never had a chance to become a professional writer, but she nonetheless wrote. She invented a character named Grandma Prairie Dog who ran a rooming house near Spur. It was typical of my mother that she would make up such a character because she was always taking in "boarders" of one kind or another. When she was a girl, she brought home injured birds, lame rabbits, and broken-backed snakes. Later on, she and my dad took in one relative after another, giving them a place to live while they finished high school or went to college. Later still, they "adopted" one Nigerian college student after another, counseling them, taking them to dinner, making our home a refuge for them. Then came the Brazilians . . .

After Taylor was born, Mom started taking in farm animals. She was determined that her granddaughter, a city kid, would have lots of critters in her life. She and my father collected geese, ducks, all kinds of chickens, even goats—and of course the dogs, Star and Boots, and their fleas. Taylor loved them all. When we visited, she always seemed to have a rooster in her hand. Grandma Latham's home was an animal boardinghouse.

In my favorite Grandma Prairie Dog story, one entitled "Pink Ice Cream," Grandma plans to give a birthday party for the Rabbit Twins. The twins wanted above all to serve pink ice cream at their party, but, ah, there was the rub. Grandma could not find any strawberries or raspberries anywhere in West Texas. She was in trouble because she couldn't stand disappointing the twins. Anything but that. So Grandma got out her red fingernail polish and painted a lightbulb. At the party, she screwed the red bulb into the overhead socket and turned on the light. Suddenly, the vanilla ice cream was pink, but also the tablecloth was pink, the napkins were pink, even the twins were pink, as well as all their guests. Grandma had saved the day— saved the birthday.

I eventually published this story in a small book that was distributed in Texas. My mother got a letter from a woman who ran a shelter for battered children. She said she regularly read the story to her damaged brood.

One little girl told her: "I wish I had a pink light all the time in my life."

So do I.

For many years, my mother lit our lives, but now that glow had gone out. Could our eyes ever adjust to another light?

10

The Brain of a Gnat

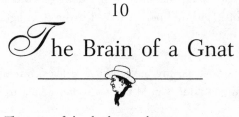

The voice of the dead was a living voice to me.
—Alfred, Lord Tennyson,
"In the Valley of Cauteretz"

Leaving Red Hill behind, Clyde turned the muddy Ford toward the very small town of Girard. He knew Gussie wanted to see her mother's grave for the first time in her life. Well, she might have seen it seventy-six years earlier, but she didn't remember seeing it. Her mom had died in the terrible influenza epidemic of 1918, when Gussie was just five years old. Her mother had been a schoolteacher. She taught the oldest of the Latham boys. It was fall—school had just started—when she caught the flu, probably from one of her students.

The whole family caught the flu, the father, mother, and all the children, including Gussie. They all went to their sickbeds except the mother, who stayed on her feet to try to take care of everybody. Of course, she was the one who never got well. That year, more Americans died from influenza on the homefront than died in the fighting on the battlefront in France. Annie Eva Boothe Willis was one of those casualties.

When they reached what had been Girard's main street, Clyde and Gussie saw the ravaged skeletons of a dead grocery and an extinct drug store. The pharmacy, made of white stucco, was missing all its doors and windows. Weeds grew up through the floorboards. The dilapidated structure stood on a lot overgrown with knee-high buffalo grass and unpleasant grassburrs called goatheads. The grocery store's front and back doors were both missing, so they could see right through the building. This long-ago market was built of wood now weathered gray. Like many buildings in the small-town West, the drug and grocery stores both had false fronts that made them look taller than they really were. Now they made the buildings look like tall shacks.

"Oh, no," Gussie said. "We used to shop there."

A little farther on, they came to the Girard cemetery, which looked to be in good health compared to the rest of town. The grass was mowed, and there were flowers on many of the graves. In case the dead got thirsty, there was a well with a large black-and-white sign: THIS CISTERN HAND DUG BY ZEAL TAYLOR IN THE EARLY 1900S. It must have taken zeal indeed. Now a windmill also watched over the dead.

"There are more people here than in town," Gussie said.

She and Clyde climbed out and got their shoes muddy, which bothered her more than it did him. The mud was a bright blood-red. Clyde and Gussie had some trouble finding her mother's grave because they expected an old, weathered headstone. Eventually they decided to check all the monuments of whatever age. They were surprised to find ANNIE EVA BOOTHE WILLIS's grave marked by a new polished-granite headstone. Neither of them had any idea who might have bought it and put it there. Somehow the blood-red earth made the grave seem more forlorn.

"This is what I came to see," Gussie said.

"That's not all you came to see," said Clyde.

"Believe whatever you like," she said. "This is why I came."

"We'll see."

Gussie's mother had been born on March 1, 1890, and died October 29, 1918, when she was just twenty-eight years old.

"I don't remember your mama," Clyde said. "I'm trying to picture her, but I just can't."

"Well, she was tall, five foot ten, and slender," said Gussie, "with long, dark hair that came down to her waist."

Gussie, who had lived almost three times as long as her mother, was crying again, as if the muddy earth needed any more watering. The wind dried the tears on her cheeks. When she could focus her eyes again, she took several pictures with her small camera. Since she was never coming back again, she wanted something to remember this place by.

Her mother's death broke up the family. The father didn't feel that he could take care of his four daughters and try to run a farm, too. So he turned his girls—Oree, Gussie, Frances, and Pauline—over to their grandma and lit out for Arizona.

"He sent Gran fifty dollars a month to help pay our

way," Gussie told Clyde. "And some more for clothes a couple of times a year."

The Willis girls' grandmother loved them and was glad to have them, but other members of the household were not so generous. Four of Granny's children, ranging in age from their teens to their early twenties, still lived with her: John, Olie, Gen, and Hool. They refused to allow the Willis girls to eat at the same table with them. These motherless girls ate at a separate orphans' table and got only the leftovers. When there was fried chicken, there was never any left by the time the platter got to the "orphans."

"We lived on biscuits and milk," Gussie remembered in the graveyard.

One afternoon, all four Willis girls were out in the cotton field hoeing when Granny appeared and wanted to chop weeds, too. She took Frances's hoe and went to work. After about ten minutes, the old woman decided she had labored long enough. She gave the hoe back to Frances and went in the house. Suddenly Gen appeared— furious, asking how the Willis girls could let their grandmother work in the field. She grabbed Frances's hoe and punched her in the stomach with the handle. The little girl doubled over in pain. Gen said she was going to kill all the Willis girls.

"I lay awake all night," Gussie told Clyde, "expecting to be murdered in my bed at any moment."

Hool used to taunt the Willis girls by claiming their father had run off to Arizona to live with a woman who had a bad reputation.

"And he called us idiots," Gussie said. "He was always calling us idiots."

"He should talk," said Clyde. "Remember the stunt he pulled with that poor horse of his?"

While he was out riding one day, Hool got mad at his horse, pulled out his six-gun, and shot the unfortunate animal right between the ears. While he was still in the saddle! That gunshot killed the horse and almost killed the rider. The horse fell on Hool, broke his leg, and pinned him down for a couple of unpleasant days until somebody finally found him.

"Hool wasn't quite as smart as a gnat," Clyde told Gussie.

On the first day of school, Gussie and the other Willis girls walked three miles to the Red Hill schoolhouse, only to find they weren't welcome there either. It was just a one-room school that taught all grades from first through eighth. The teacher looked at the four new arrivals and announced that there wasn't room for them.

"She said the only way we could stay," Gussie told Clyde, "would be if she could hang us up by our toes."

"Like bats?" he said.

"I guess."

Since the local school wouldn't have them, the girls had to find a new place to live. They were passed on to other relatives who didn't want them either, first in the small town of Dickens, later in the smaller town of Roaring Springs. But at least these four cotton-pickin', West Texas Cinderellas could go to school.

11

I Remember Mama

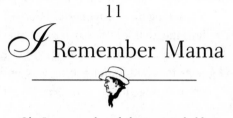

Oh, I am a cook and the captain bold.
—Sir William Schwenck Gilbert,
  "The Yarn of the *Nancy Belle," The "Bab" Ballads*

While my father continued to explore the landscape of the past with Gussie, I roamed an inner landscape with my mother. Sitting at my keyboard typing dialogue, I remembered that my mother's heroes had always been writers: Zane Grey, Gene Stratton Porter, Jack London, Shakespeare. Of course, I wanted to be one of my mom's heroes, too, so there was nothing for it except to become a writer myself. The ultimate would be someday to write about her.

One day I came home from first grade and cried to her that a second grader was picking on me. She told me to go to school tomorrow, pick a fight with the bully, and lick him good. Since I usually did what my mother said, I beat the shit out of the big second grader. Afterward I had no trouble from him. Sitting at my desk, so many years later, I still found it hard to believe that I had attacked that mountain of a second grader. What got into me? In a word: Mom.

I remembered her comforting me when the goat ate my kite . . . her teaching me the names of hundreds of birds . . . her telling me that FDR was a great president no matter what some of our relatives said . . . her taking ho-hum good grades for granted but getting very upset at bad ones . . . her painting birds . . . her gardening . . . her cooking . . .

Well, actually, she wasn't a very good cook. I was the only person I know who loved the food at college. While I was working at *New York* magazine, I got into an argument with the writer Richard Reeves over whose mom cooked worse. We made a real contest of it. People gathered around to listen. I said my mother was such a bad cook that she once opened a can of ham, plopped it uncooked onto a platter, and served it to the Methodist minister and his wife for Sunday dinner. The jelly on the ham was still quivering. Richard said his mother was such a bad cook that she opened a can of beans, poured them cold into a bowl, and served them to his fiancée when he brought her home to meet the family. That was all she served. Everybody agreed that Richard won the contest, but I was a close second. My mother didn't care that she wasn't a good cook, didn't want to cook well, had better things to do. Like painting, writing, teaching. My dad was the good cook in the family.

While I was reminiscing, my wife came home. She isn't much of a cook either. Oh, she is a good cook when she wants to be, but she prefers to eat out or order in. Like my mother, she has better things to do. Like cover the White House or interview Robert Redford.

"What's the matter?" Lesley asked.

"Nothing." I said. "I was just thinking about my mom and how she couldn't cook."

"And that's upset you? Don't be silly. She didn't want to be a good cook. That's what makes your mom different from most. Yours didn't cook and didn't give guilt. Most do both. I wonder what the connection is between cooking and guilt."

"Must be one. Some law of nature."

"Absolutely. Where do you want to order from tonight?"

12

*O*edipus in Spur

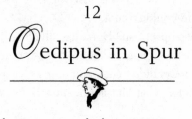

O bury me not on the lone prairie
Where the wild coyotes will howl o'er me.
—"The Dying Cowboy"

As Clyde and Gussie were leaving Girard—still holding hands—they drove by the "Boothe house," where her mother's parents had lived. Only the house wasn't there any more. Clyde also showed Gussie where the railroad tracks had once been. She used to ride the train to what was then the thriving small city of Spur, where she shopped (most of the stores now gone), visited up and down crowded Main Street (now empty), and went to the picture show (now closed).

"We all come down here one day to meet my brother Glenn," Clyde told Gussie. "Looking down the track, we saw the smoke, but the train just didn't get there. We waited and waited. Turned out the train jumped the track. Again. We called it the Wooden-Axle Railroad. Remember?"

"Now that you mention it, I do."

Then Clyde and Gussie headed for Jayton (population 553), thirty miles away in Kent County—named after Andrew Kent, who was killed in the Alamo. A man they called Uncle Rob had been sheriff there for twenty-three years.

As they drove along, Gussie, eighty-one, and Clyde, eighty-four, told each other why they would never get married again. Never. No doubt at all. They were too old for such shenanigans. Besides, their lives were just fine the way they were.

Clyde told her that he went to the drugstore, Dan's Pharmacy, every morning for coffee with the men of the town. Then he played golf with some of those same friends at the bedraggled but nonetheless impressive-for-Spur nine-hole golf course. In the afternoons, he went for drives by himself. He was doing real good, thank you. He didn't need any more.

Gussie told Clyde that she played bridge as regularly as he played golf. She was content, too. She didn't need any more either. Don't worry about her. No, sir.

Well, don't worry about him either. No sirree bob.

"Did I ever tell you about the meanest man in West Texas?" Clyde asked, changing the subject. They had talked about marriage long enough.

"No," said Gussie.

"Well, us boys, we'd been down in the canyons chopping a load of wood. Stealing it really. Cedar mostly. Smelled real good. We hauled it home, and pretty soon here come the meanest man in West Texas. His name was Robertson and he was one of the last cowboys to wear a six-gun strapped to his leg. He was on horseback, and he'd been tracking us. Pop saw him coming a long way off. He told Mom'n us boys to stay away from the windows. Then he opened a window and propped up a shotgun so the barrel was sticking out over the windowsill. Making sure it was real visible."

Clyde laughed.

"When Robertson rode up, Pop went out to meet him. This mean old cowboy kept looking over Pop's shoulder at that gun sticking out the window. Pop and Robertson just chatted about the weather and how much we needed rain—and then the meanest man in West Texas just rode off."

"Thank goodness."

"Coupla years later, a man walked into the Spur cafe and shot old Robertson in the stomach in the middle of lunch. He never ate another meal."

"Oh, no."

"Nobody missed him. Except maybe the waitress who never got her tip that day."

"Well, he probably wasn't a big tipper anyway."

Clyde laughed. He enjoyed laughing—especially laughing with his houseguest. She really was amusing.

Reaching Jayton, they visited another cemetery because Gussie wanted to see where her grandmother was buried. The place was well tended with broad gravel avenues. There were no weeds in sight and plenty of flowers. The ground was so utterly flat that it looked like a tabletop with dominoes (the tombstones) set up for a game. One of those stones bore the name CHISOM, as in: "Come along, boys, and listen to my tale, I'll tell you of my troubles on the old . . ."

Gussie found her grandmother's grave near the center of the cemetery. Its headstone was weathered. Flowers bloomed in a clay pot beside the stone. The grave itself was covered with white pebbles. Her son John—who was shot behind the ear when he tried to break up a poker game—lay next to her.

Clyde's mother, Sally Harriet, was buried nearby while his father, John Henry, was consigned to a far-off plot in a lonely corner of the graveyard. Clyde hadn't wanted his dad lying next to his mom because of the way he had treated her. One day, Clyde had come home and found his father chasing his mother with a butcher knife. The strapping son, protecting his mother, took the knife away from his father, threw him out of the house, and told him never to come back. He never did. Oedipus comes to Spur.

After visiting the graves and taking more pictures, Gussie and Clyde drove through the small town of Jayton, past dead stores with tin roofs rolling up like the tops of sardine cans. Prickly pears lined Main Street. A television antenna hitchhiked on the Jayton water tower. The old, deserted Jayton hotel, with its tiers of round-topped doors, looked like a tumbledown birdhouse. The town wasn't nearly as well kept up as the graveyard.

Having seen and felt enough for one day, Clyde and Gussie returned to Spur tired and ready for bed. She was still nervous about fleas. He was nervous because she was. They said a very nervous good night to each other and then both lay awake in spite of their fatigue.

That night the wind blew and the fleas didn't bite.

$\mathcal{P}$alominos in the Living Room

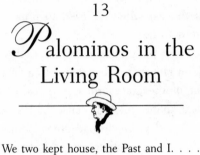

We two kept house, the Past and I. . . .
—Thomas Hardy,
"The Ghost of the Past"

On Saturday, their second full day together, Gussie and Clyde went for another hand-holding drive. She wore her second outfit (number two out of four), a denim dress with a red belt and red shoes. This time they headed north. Eleven miles later, they reached Dickens, the county seat, population 322. Gussie found Dickens depressing. It used to have not only more people but actual stores. The town seemed to have dried up and blown away, like so many of the farmers.

Gussie, who had attended grades one, two, and three in Dickens, wanted to go by her old schoolhouse. It wasn't there. The wind fluttered the weeds where it had been. The Dickens courthouse still looked impressive, but it was now surrounded by shacks that lawyers used for offices.

These buildings looked like something sharecroppers wouldn't live in. The jail resembled a large tombstone. It wasn't until you got close that you realized that there were small windows with heavy grates over them. The light of day would have a very hard time breaking into that jail.

They parked near the courthouse and Clyde hunted up some people to introduce to Gussie. He obviously loved these introductions. He was proud of his visitor. Of course, everybody wanted to know how long she was staying.

"I've got to go back day after tomorrow," Gussie said over and over. "I only packed enough clothes for four days."

Then the Dickensians all told her the same thing: Gussie, you've got to stay for homecoming. It was only a week away.

"Well, if I stay," she said, "I'll just have to go to homecoming naked. That's all."

*B*ack on the road, Clyde and Gussie headed for Roaring Springs, where she had attended fourth, fifth, and sixth grades. The town had once been roaring but not anymore. She was moderately happy to find her old schoolhouse still standing—but it wasn't used any longer. It was a ghost school.

Then they drove by the home where Gussie had lived with her Aunt Willie and Uncle Frank. They already had four children of their own and always made the Willis girls feel like intruders. Still, Gussie was glad—and surprised—to see the house still standing. But now it was lived in by a couple of horses. There were palominos in the living room.

"You *all* lived in that little house?" asked Clyde, knowing the answer.

"We certainly did, and there were nine of us," said Gussie. "In just two rooms. There was the living room—and we had two beds in there. My aunt and uncle slept in one of those beds, and my two girl cousins slept in the other. The only other room was the kitchen—just a kind of lean-to built onto the house. And they'd partitioned off part of it to make this little-bitty bedroom with one bed. That's where I slept with my two sisters. Right out the kitchen door, they had a storm cellar—my two boy cousins slept there. Underground."

"And I thought we were crowded."

"We had togetherness."

They both laughed remembering those days and that lost world of youth and hardship.

"We had four rooms," Clyde said. "One of them was the dining room, and one of them was the kitchen. So that left the living room and the other room. During one time, they was five of us plus Mom and Pop—"

"But there were six of you boys?"

"That was before Chick was born. Anyway, they was seven of us all together, and then here come Granddad Latham and Granny Fat looking for a place to stay. She was just a little woman, but we always called her Granny Fat. I think she must've been fat at one time, but not anymore. Anyway they moved in with us, and they had two granddaughters that they was raising."

Gussie missed a lot that used to be there, but she could see some improvement since her day. The few remaining farmhouses did have indoor plumbing. No more fragrant outhouses in the backyard. That was a part of her growing up that she didn't miss.

"There's something I never could forgive Pop for," Clyde said.

"What?" asked Gussie.

"Remember that time you girls walked three miles to play with us boys? Then when you got there, Pop told you to just turn around and go back home."

"Sure. You'd built this playhouse, you and Abo. And you asked us to come play in it."

"And Pop wouldn't let you. I'm gettin' mad at him all over again just rememberin'."

They rode in silence for a few minutes, which was unusual for them. Clyde was reliving his anger toward his dad. A mean man.

"I'll tell you what let's do," Clyde said, cheering up. "Let's go out to the Pitchfork and eat lunch with the cowboys."

"That sounds nice," said Gussie.

Rolling along, Clyde and Gussie once again told each other that they would never marry. They were both content with their lives as they were. They were both doing just fine.

14
Teacher

And gladly wolde she lerne, and gladly teche.
—Chaucer, *The Canterbury Tales*

All the Lathams called my mother Teacher. Spur was the kind of small Texas town that just loved sobriquets. Clyde was called Dub. Most of his brothers had nicknames, too. Albert was either Abo or Bit, because he was a runt. Francis was Chick because he woke up one morning with a feather—from his feather pillow—in his hair. John was Mutt because he was tall and had a short friend, just like those funny-papers characters Mutt and Jeff. The boys had a good friend who never closed his mouth, so they called him Fly Trap.

But why did they call my mother Teacher? Why did they name her after her job? There were cowpunchers in the family, but nobody called them Cowboy. There were clodhoppers, but nobody named them Farmer. There were layabouts, but nobody called them Bum. They referred to my mother as Teacher because they were so amazed to have an actual educator in the family.

Teacher started teaching in a one-room schoolhouse. She was eighteen years old and smaller than some of her students. One of the big boys tried to push her around. Terrified, she grabbed a post and beat him silly. She didn't have any serious discipline problems after that.

*M*y mom and dad knew each other from the beginning of time, at least time as they knew it. When he proposed, she turned him down. Then she had second thoughts and wrote him a letter telling him she had changed her mind. They were married on June 25, 1939. Clyde served on Trinidad during the early years of World War II, helping guard the Caribbean. By 1943, he was back in Spur, where I was born in October.

Since the town was having trouble finding teachers, the school board came out to see my father. They asked if he would be willing to help them out by teaching for a while. It was either teach or farm, so he said he'd teach. The job turned out to be a little more than that: Clyde was teacher, principal, bus driver, and coach. He coached six-man football, track, and boys and girls basketball. It was still easier than farming.

*I*n 1946, we lived in a schoolhouse. At the time, there was a severe postwar housing shortage. The small town of Munday wanted to hire my father as its coach, and he wanted to take the job, because it would give him a chance to coach eleven-man football. But he couldn't find a place for us to live. Reluctantly, he had to turn down the offer.

"Wait a minute, not so fast," said the superintendent.

"We've got some empty classrooms. You can live in one of them."

So the three of us (my sister hadn't arrived yet) moved into a new one-room home that came equipped with blackboards. The desks came out—and in went beds, a couch, coffee tables, a stove, and even a refrigerator.

I wasted no time in getting into trouble. One night, the three-year-old version of me slipped out of our classroom and headed for the lunchroom. I had decided to stage a boxing match in the gymnasium upstairs, but I needed combatants. For some reason, clear to a three-year-old, I decided food should do the fighting. So I diligently went to work carrying all the canned goods in the cafeteria upstairs to the gym, where I placed them inside the boxing ring. This battle was to give new meaning to the expression "food fight."

The next morning, everybody got mad. The cafeteria was mad because it didn't have any food to feed to its students. The phys ed department was mad because it couldn't use its boxing ring. And my father was mad be-cause—well, he was mad.

My daughter loves to hear me tell this tale. She adores stories about her father screwing up.

𝒥 wasn't much taller than a football when I started working out with my dad's football teams. I would suit up with them on game days and sit beside my father on the bench. For a long time, I thought jockstraps were defec-tive underwear, another result of postwar shortages.

As a coach, my dad believed in all sorts of psychological treats and tricks. Before one important game, he persuaded the school board to buy the team new uniforms to improve their self-image. Munday won. In a game for the bi-district championship, he saw that his boys were struggling, so he told his star player to pretend to pass out and fall over. This "injury" fired up the team, and they won bi-district.

My father lost only a handful of games during his years as the Munday coach.

Then our family moved down to DeLeon, and our fortunes changed. The high-school kids went out for band instead of football. My dad had only ten players part of the time. Making matters worse, the coach before him had run the score up on all the other teams around there. Every time DeLeon played one of those towns, the opposing coaches would apologize ahead of time. They would say: We're sorry, but we're gonna beat you all we can.

"And they did too," my father would say, telling the tale.

I hated that particular story. As I've said, I couldn't stand the thought of my father getting beaten once, much less over and over.

*W*hen I was old enough to start school, I lived in fear that I might someday be in my mom's class. It never happened. We played tackle football at recess and went to school barefoot when the weather was warm enough.

Much later, I realized that I would've been lucky to have my mother for a teacher, because she emphasized reading and writing. (She taught math, too, of course, but it didn't really interest her.) Her students spent most of their time reading, summarizing, and then analyzing. That's how she taught English. That's how she taught social studies. That's how she taught history. That's even how she taught science. I first encountered such training in college.

Written like a son? Well, I hope so.

Recently, when I did some teaching myself at the University of Southern California film school, I called my dad to tell him how much I enjoyed the exercise. I was really stunned at how much I loved running a class.

"What a surprise," said my father. "Did you forget that your parents were both teachers?"

$\mathcal{D}$on't Scare Gussie Off

Foot in the stirrup and hand on the horn,
Best damned cowboy ever was born.
　　　　　　—"The Old Chisholm Trail"

The Pitchfork sprawls over broken country about thirty miles northeast of Spur. The ranch was founded by a bookkeeper turned cowboy turned rancher. It is one of the last spreads in the old tradition, with a bunkhouse, a chuck wagon, and ranching carried on very much the way it was over a hundred years ago. Except they sometimes use planes and helicopters. The brand is an upside-down pitchfork with three prongs, which looks like the Greek letter psi: $\sqcup$.

The ranch is managed by Bob Moorhouse, who attends my father's church. He regularly turns up for services wearing a cowboy shirt, jeans stuffed inside boots that stop just below his kneecaps, and of course spurs. He also wears a bushy, 1880s mustache that hides his upper lip.

Moorhouse takes ranch and cowboy traditions very seriously, almost reverently. He enforces a cowboy dress code at the Pitchfork Ranch from the crown of the ten-gallon hats his "boys" wear down to the jingling of the rowels of their spurs. The cowpokes at other ranches sometimes wear Nike running shoes and baseball caps, but not at the Pitchfork. Moorhouse believes being a cowboy is a sacred trust. Treating it otherwise would let down old Charles Goodnight, Billy, Wild Bill, Jesse and Frank, Butch and Sundance, the Wild Bunch, the whole Hole in the Wall Gang, and all the other ghosts of the West.

Clyde and Gussie arrived just as the cook was ringing the come-and-get-it bell. They parked near the cookhouse, which stands by itself a hundred feet from the big ranch house. Sandy-haired Bob Moorhouse and his raven-maned wife, Linda, came out to meet them. Clyde proudly introduced Gussie. Then they all went into the cookhouse together. They sat down on benches at a long white table in a white room. There were eight or nine cowboys already seated at the table. They gather here for three meals a day. And every meal always includes beans, biscuits, and beef. The most picturesque of the Pitchfork's time-warp cowhands wore chaps, leather cuffs, and a leather collar.

"Bob, tell Gussie how many windmills you've got," Clyde said.

"Well, we've got a hundred and thirteen," Moorhouse said. "We've got a cowboy, his full-time job's just ridin' herd on all those windmills. Keepin' 'em turnin' and pumpin'."

"How many horses do you have?" asked Gussie.

"Let's see, we've got seventy-five in the mare herd. And we've got a hundred and thirty saddle horses. About two hundred in all."

"How many cows?"

"We've got about five thousand mother cows."

"How many cowboys?"

"Usually around a dozen."

"We liked to've had one fewer cowboy today," said James, the foreman, from the other end of the table.

"What happened?" asked Gussie.

"This mornin', I looked over at Charlie here, and he was doin' this dance. I thought it was St. Vitus' dance. Or maybe he was on fire. Figured he musta been burnin'—goin' up in actual flames—to jump around like that. Turned out, what happened was, a tarantula run up his leg."

"I'd rather have a rattlesnake up my leg," said poor Charlie.

"Now that tarantula never hurt you," said the foreman, "but you like to hurt yourself havin' a fit like that."

"Give me a rattlesnake any day."

"Come on, boys," said Linda Moorhouse. "Enough about spiders and snakes. We don't wanta scare Gussie off."

"No, we certainly do not," said Clyde.

𝒪n the ride home from lunch with the cowboys, Gussie found herself thinking about her father, who had been a cowboy of sorts. He learned how on Granny Goodall-Adams's place, where he helped herd her hundred head of cattle.

When he went out to Arizona—leaving his girls behind—Fred Willis became a cowboy of a different sort. Instead of punching cattle, he poisoned coyotes, for $150 a month. The ranchers had complained to the government that these varmints were killing their calves, so the government hired Gussie's father to kill the killers. Back then, people had few qualms about making war on predators.

"He lived in his truck," Gussie told Clyde. "He had a pickup fixed with his bed in there and his camping gear and his cooking utensils. He traveled from ranch to ranch in Arizona and poisoned coyotes. That was his job. Then on the weekends he'd go into one of the towns and rent a room in a hotel. And get a bath and shave and everything. He took a bath once a week, whether he needed it or not."

"Well, you didn't need one way out like that," Clyde said. "Nobody to smell you."

"I guess not. Well, he could play any musical instrument. In the evening he'd play solitaire and play his Jew's harp, his harmonica, his violin."

"I didn't know he was a fiddler."

"Oh, yes." Gussie smiled. "He'd fiddle and sing all by himself. So that was his entertainment during the week."

"Musta been lonely," Clyde said with feeling, already anticipating the loneliness after Gussie went back home. "How'd he stand it?"

"Well, on weekends"—Gussie smiled—"he had lady friends in every one of those little towns. That probably helped."

"You know Pop and Rob Goodall were fiddlers, too." Clyde smiled too. "They'd fiddle all over this country for dances. They'd put their fiddles in flour sacks and tie them to the horns of their saddles. And here they'd go."

Come live with me and be my love . . .

16

The Friendly Funeral Home

"A loaf of bread," the Walrus said,
"Is what we chiefly need:
Pepper and vinegar besides
Are very good indeed—
Now, if you're ready, Oysters dear,
We can begin to feed."
—Lewis Carroll,
"The Walrus and the Carpenter"

On Sunday, their third full day together, Clyde drove Gussie down to see the town of Post, population almost 3,320. She wore her next-to-last outfit—a paisley print dress. For her, having to go naked was just around the corner, just one outfit away. All she had left in her suitcase was a pair of black slacks and a blouse. Tomorrow she would put those on and catch the plane. But today she had Post to see.

Gussie was favorably impressed by Post: Maybe West Texas towns weren't quite so bad after all. While Dickens, Roaring Springs, and even Spur had dried up and were blowing away, Post didn't need to worry about such a wind. Gussie was happy to see construction going on all over town. There were people on the streets. And there were restaurants.

Clyde and Gussie stopped to eat at a restaurant with a pretty name: the Chaparral. It looked good outside and inside. Gussie could almost have been back in Sacramento. (Except three cowboys came in for lunch wearing spurs that jingled.) They both ordered steak—this was ranching country, after all—and big baked potatoes. Gussie was pleasantly surprised to find cheese at the center of the rolls. Clyde introduced her to everybody in the Chaparral, and they all told her she had to stay for homecoming. No, sorry, no clothes, no way.

When they got home to Spur's unbustling streets, Gussie missed Post. But the town wasn't completely deserted. Happily, there was the occasional person actually walking on the sidewalks in front of the town's mostly empty stores. And Clyde introduced her to them all—introduced her to people she had already met—and was as always proud to do so. There was more idle talk about staying for homecoming, but Gussie brushed it aside.

Then Clyde parked the car in front of Spur's funeral home, which has a wide front porch held up by four white columns. It is located right on Main Street next door to the Methodist church. Shaded by tall, bushy trees, this "home" looks much like any other house, except it has a sign out front that says:

CAMPBELL'S
FUNERAL
HOME

Bill Campbell, the town mortician, and Stacy, his wife, are among my father's best friends. Bill recently came very close to needing some of his own services, but quadruple-bypass heart surgery saved his life just in time. He is about five feet, nine inches with a round, open face and a slightly rounded body. He has a knack for putting people at their ease in the most trying of situations. His wife, Stacy, is beautiful—almost too beautiful for Spur and its untrodden ways. She has light brown hair and lots of optimistic energy. A violet by a mossy stone half hidden from the eye. Stacy and Bill don't seem like undertakers.

Nonetheless, the funeral home was literally their home for years, but recently they bought a new house and moved out of the "home." They no longer sleep under the same roof as corpses and caskets.

Clyde loves to drop by this death house for lively visits. And he isn't the only one. Stacy and Bill are among the most popular couples in town. She met him when he was in mortuary school. Now they have two children, Kyla, twelve, and Spence, ten. Since Spur is literally a dying town, Campbell's Funeral Home is a growth industry. This was where my mother's body was prepared for burial.

When Clyde and Gussie got out of the car, Spence came running up to them, the wind mussing his hair. Gussie grabbed him and kissed him on the cheek, leaving red lips. Then his mom came running up and kissed him on the other cheek, leaving another set of lips. Spence, who looked like a wild Indian in warpaint, turned and ran to put a stop to all this kissing. Unfortunately, the fleeing boy almost knocked over an elderly woman named Dorothy, who was just leaving the corpse shop.

"Excuse me," Spence said formally.

"No harm done, young man," said old Dorothy. "But you can do me a favor—if you'd be so kind."

"Sure. What?"

"When I die, just don't let your daddy put no pantyhose on me. I hate those things. You'll remember?"

"Yes, ma'am," said Spence, running again. He got away this time.

Stacy invited Clyde and Gussie inside. They sat down in the office, where, two years earlier, almost to the day, we had ordered a casket for my mother.

Gussie couldn't help noticing that Stacy was looking her over very, very carefully. As a newcomer, she had no way of knowing that this young woman had been one of my mother's closest friends. I still remember the mortician's wife crying all through the funeral. Mom was over a generation older than Stacy, but they connected in a way that was direct, warm, very special, even spiritual. Now Stacy was not happy to see somebody showing up to try to take my mother's place. As if Holmes were auditioning a new Watson, Jack looking for a new Jill, Clyde trying out a new Bonnie.

Stacy stared at Gussie, but she didn't talk to her. She spoke exclusively to Clyde, as if Gussie weren't there at all. Gussie thought: Okay, child, it's all right with me if you want to ignore me, I'll just ignore you, too. Gussie turned to Stacy's father, Travis Hoover, who happened to be visiting, and talked to him as if his daughter weren't there. Two could play that game.

"How long has it been since you've seen Spur?" asked Stacy's dad.

"I left here in 1927," Gussie said. "My father got remarried and asked us to come out to Arizona and live with him. I was fourteen. I haven't been back since. That's sixty-seven years."

Naturally, Travis asked Gussie if she was going to stay over for homecoming.

No, not at all, her mind and her suitcase were already made up. She was definitely going home in the morning.

*B*ut that evening, Gussie called her daughter, Nola, who lives with her family in the redwood forests of Boulder Creek, California, and told her that everybody wanted her to stay over for homecoming. Nola, who didn't hear the usual depression in her mom's voice, encouraged her to stay. But Gussie reminded Nola that she had packed clothes for only four days.

"Well, just go downtown and buy some new clothes," Nola advised a little sharply.

"You've never been to Spur," Gussie said.

Then Clyde and Gussie settled down in their side-by-side reclining easy chairs. When my mother was alive, these chairs had a small coffee table between them, but now Clyde had removed the table and pushed the chairs so close they were touching.

One last time, Clyde decided to try to convince Gussie to stay a little longer. He argued that not only he but also the combined populations of Spur, Dickens, Jayton, Post, Roaring Springs, and the Pitchfork Land and Cattle Company wanted her to stay put, at least until after homecoming.

"All right," Gussie said, "I'll stay if you'll promise me one thing."

"I'll promise you anything," Clyde said.

"Promise to get a girlfriend after I go. You enjoy a woman's company so much."

"I promise."

"Good, I'll stay."

When Gussie called home to tell her children—Nola and Fred—they were not only pleased but also stunned. They had never known their mother to outstay her packing before. And staying for homecoming meant remaining in Spur not just a couple of days but a whole extra week. Instead of leaving on Monday the 10th, she would go on Monday the 17th of October.

Nola asked her mother what she was doing for clothes. Gussie assured her daughter that she would be able to mix and match and come up with all sorts of different outfits. Nola began to think that something serious was going on.

I continued to call my dad every night. One evening I asked him innocently enough: "What're you doing?"

"Just sittin' here holding hands with Gussie," he said.

So I too began to suspect that something important might be happening. Of course, I still had reservations. The longer Gussie stayed, the more heartbreaking the parting would be. Why couldn't she have just minded her own business and stayed home in Sacramento, where she belonged?

Come live with me and be my love; and we will all the pleasures prove . . .

$\mathcal{Q}$ueen of the South Plains

Never play cards with a man called Doc. Never eat at a place called Mom's. Never sleep with a woman whose troubles are worse than your own.

—Nelson Algren

They fell into a routine. Holding hands in the car. Holding hands in their recliners. Holding hands at the Dairy Queen every day at lunchtime.

The DQ is an institution in West Texas: the Queen of the South Plains. It is the only restaurant in many little West Texas towns, including Spur. Other cafes do occasionally sprout up, but they're like tumbleweeds, soon breaking loose and blowing away. The Dairy Queens are as firmly rooted as the mesquites that go on forever. This Queen is to Spur what the saloon with its swinging doors used to be: a place where people get together and socialize. Just fewer gunfights.

But the first time Gussie walked into the Dairy Queen, ushered in by Clyde, she wasn't impressed. She thought:

Thank heavens I don't live here. Really. With the Dairy Queen the only decent restaurant! Sacramento had hundreds of restaurants to choose from.

The people she met at the DQ—Clyde introduced everybody who came through the door—were very nice. They embodied the friendliness of these wide-open spaces, where strangers had been welcome from time immemorial because the pioneer settlers were so lonely. Strangers brought news, gossip, human contact. Now that tradition had been handed down to the Dairy Queen, where Gussie was the stranger who was now made very, very welcome.

She studied the place. Half the men were wearing cowboy hats, the other half baseball caps. The sheriff sat at a large table in the middle of the dining room, wearing his six-gun like an old-time gunfighter. At the far end of the room stood a case displaying Spur's many polo trophies. Polo-playing cowboys, riding western saddles, regularly defeated fancy eastern teams riding English.

"Did you ever play polo?" Gussie asked.

"We used to try to play it when we was kids," Clyde said. "Back then, we thought there wasn't anything we couldn't do on a horse."

"I'll bet."

"We'd go to the show Friday night or Saturday. And they was always about cowboys. So on Sunday, we'd all go down to the canyons, and we'd try to do what they did. Ride under a tree and get knocked off."

Gussie laughed.

"We'd get the horse to running and then we'd jump on it. Once there was some girls along, so I decided to show off. I got my little old horse running, and then I stepped off him. The girth broke and the stirrup hit me right in the forehead."

Gussie laughed again. She loved the way Clyde's stories so often ended with the joke on him. She could just see that stirrup whacking him right between the eyes. Yes, she was having a good time, but she thanked heaven she didn't live here in Spur. Not with the Dairy Queen the only restaurant.

When I called that night, my father sounded almost too happy. The happier he was now, the sadder he would be later, right?

"The folks around here have really taken to Gussie," said my dad. "She fits in just perfect. Like she'd never left. Ever'body wants to know why she has to go home after homecoming. Ever'body says she should stay longer."

I thought: Oh, no.

Come live with me and be my love; and we will all the pleasures prove that valleys, groves, hills, and fields . . .

18

$\mathcal{O}$ Brave Old World

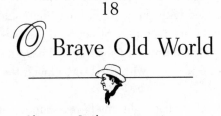

Oh, young Lochinvar is coming;
Though his hair is getting grey.
—Anonymous,
"A Strike Among the Poets"

It was Wednesday evening. Gussie's extra week in Spur was passing all too fast. The first time she had left this part of the country, she had been happy to put it behind her. Happy to think she would never come back. Never ever and good riddance. But now she was reluctant to go. And she couldn't quite believe it.

Clyde and Gussie sat side by side in their recliners, holding hands. The wind moaned outside. He had something he wanted to say, but he was a little nervous. He really had believed that his solitary life was fine, but now he knew better. Holding Gussie's hand, he could feel his palm sweating. He wondered if she could feel it too. He wasn't a shy man, not at all, but he was having trouble finding his voice. Eventually it turned up.

"Gussie, I love you," Clyde said.

She was shocked. She hadn't expected him to say it. She hadn't expected him to feel it. He was eighty-four years old. She was eighty-one. They should have left romantic love behind them a long time ago. It just wasn't dignified, not ladylike, not at their age. But appropriate or not, undignified or whatever, she was feeling something too, and it felt good. O brave new world that has such people in it.

"I love you, too," Gussie said, startling herself.

Those two sentences, the one he said, the one she said, changed her whole sense of herself. Her whole definition of who she was. Her hopes and expectations. She wasn't coming to the end of something. She was starting a whole new life. Clyde said those three magic words and changed Gussie into a new woman. Of course, by saying the words he changed himself too. O brave new pretty old world.

Teenagers ask themselves if something as wonderful as falling in love will ever happen to them. It hasn't yet. Maybe it never will. Then when it does, when they fall in love for the first time, this falling seems like a miracle. Yes, it did happen to them! Yes! Yes! They can hardly believe their good fortune. At the other end of life, Gussie and Clyde felt the same way. They never thought they would ever fall in love again. And now that they had, it felt like a miracle. Yes, it had really happened! They could hardly believe their luck. They were both in a state of wonder.

Of course, for a love story to be a truly romantic love story, it must overcome barriers. Love that is easy, that leaps no fences, that climbs over no barricade, may be real love, but it isn't the stuff that great love stories are made of. In England in the good old days, the class system erected wonderful barriers to love and writers profited. Jane Austen gave us Elizabeth Bennet, who leapt over the class hurdle to marry Mr. Darcy. Charlotte Brontë contributed a governess named Jane Eyre, who fell in love with Mr. Rochester, the master of the house, and got her man. D. H. Lawrence presented us with Lady Chatterley and her gamekeeper. In Italy, or rather Shakespeare's version of Italy, the Montagues and the Capulets tried to interpose a moat between Romeo and Juliet. But in modern-day America there are so few barriers of class or whatever that we have a dearth of romantic love stories. It's just too damn easy.

But then comes age. Age is the last true barrier to romantic love. And now Clyde and Gussie had overcome that barrier.

Which was fine, which was great, so long as nobody got badly hurt. At his age, how resilient could my father be?

Come live with me and be my love, and we will all the pleasures prove that valleys, groves, hills, and fields, woods, or steepy mountain yields.

19
What Are You Doing?

Then come kiss me, sweet and twenty,
Youth's a stuff will not endure.
      —Shakespeare, *Twelfth Night*

Clyde pulled the old Ford over to the side of the road and stopped.

"Why are we stopping?" Gussie asked. "I hope you don't expect me to pick any more cotton. I'm telling you, my cotton-picking days are over. Maybe I'll even give up wearing cotton—now that I know what terrible things they do to it!"

"No, I'm not interested in cotton," Clyde said, "not at the moment anyhow."

He put his arms around her and kissed her. Then he touched her.

"What are you doing?" she asked—startled.

"Gussie, I've loved you," he said, "since you were three years old."

Clyde kissed her again, this time longer. And again. Longer still. The wind howled outside the car.

"You're acting like a teenager," Gussie said.

"What's wrong with that?" Clyde asked.

She considered the question for a moment.

"Nothing," she decided.

"Why should teenagers have all the fun?" he asked. "We deserve it as much as they do. More. We've earned it."

They kissed and hugged and touched again.

"I've heard of old folks falling into a second childhood," Gussie said, "but this feels like a second adolescence. Doesn't it?"

"It just feels good," Clyde said.

The next day, they drove out into the country again, parked again, and necked again. It was a pretty old world.

And we will sit upon the rocks . . .

20
Now and Then

Time present and time past
Are both perhaps present in time future,
And time future contained in time past.
— T. S. Eliot, "Burnt Norton"

On the weekend of the 15th and 16th, there were all sorts
of homecoming events all over the country, but Clyde and
Gussie went to only one, the parade. This business about
staying for homecoming had never really been about
homecoming, had it?

On Saturday, parade day, Clyde said they would be
smart to get an early start. So while the sun was still low,
they climbed in his old Ford, drove down to Main Street,
and parked.

Clyde and Gussie were reenacting a long-dead weekend
ritual. In the old days, when Spur was the center of a busy
agricultural community, the crowds descended on the
town every Saturday. And again the wise came early to be
sure they found a prized parking place on Main Street.

Originally, farmers drove into town in buggies or hacks or surreys or rattling buckboards. Later on, they drove Model T Fords, later still, Model A's. They came to Spur ready to spend the day shopping, visiting, gossiping. Main Street was a party several blocks long. When they were exhausted, the people would return to their parked buggies or cars or whatever to rest up. Then, refreshed, they would head back out into the party again. It was a weekly festival that included all ages: babes in arms, kids, teenagers, parents, grandparents, even great-grandparents. Then that whole world dried up and blew away.

Nor were Clyde and Gussie the only ones who came early to find good parking places. Lots of folks were reenacting that old tradition today. Main Street was soon lined with cars and pickups from one end to the other.

"It's good to see Spur busy again," Gussie said.

"Yeah, it is," said Clyde. "Course, they're doin' all this just for you. If you'd gone home, they'd've canceled the parade."

"Then Spur owes me a vote of thanks, doesn't it?"

"I'll say."

Looking out at a teeming Main Street, Gussie and Clyde both saw in the Spur of today the Spur of yesterday. Just as they saw in each other the way they were now and the way they used to be. The one superimposed upon the other. Yesterday and today swirling in a kind of dance, a slow dance, a romantic dance. Bodies swayed to music. New bodies and old bodies. Brightening glances. Eyes bright then and still bright now. How can you tell the present from the past?

Once again, Main Street was one long party. People

kept dropping by the old Ford to visit and gossip. Clyde proudly introduced Gussie to lots of new folks. One old man remembered buying a horse from her father seventy years ago. Good horse.

"Clyde, my hand hurts," Gussie said.

"What's the matter?" asked Clyde.

"I've shaken every single hand in Spur."

The parade started and gave Gussie's aching hand a rest. Clyde's nephew Tommy Latham rode by on a fire truck. He was a handyman and a volunteer firefighter. Tommy turned on the siren and frightened all the horses.

And we will sit upon the rocks, seeing the shepherds feed their flocks . . .

21

You Can't Do That!

Come, my Celia, let us prove,
While we can, the sports of love;
Time will not be ours forever,
He at length our good will sever.
Spend not, then, his gifts, in vain;
Suns that set may rise again,
But if once we lose this light,
'Tis with us perpetual night.
—Ben Jonson,
"Come, My Celia"

Monday morning, October 17th, the morning she was
scheduled to fly back to California, Gussie announced
that she was nervous about changing planes in Dallas.
Clyde, delighted, offered to drive her from Spur to Big D
so she could take a direct flight back to Sacramento. It
would mean about ten hours in the car, but he certainly
wouldn't mind spending some extra time with Gussie. She
said she would think it over. She thought. She said yes.
Gas up the car.

Then Stacy came to see her.

"I don't think Clyde is up to a trip like that," the undertaker's wife said solemnly.

Gussie wanted to say: So now you want to talk to me. Because you're afraid I'm going to steal your handsome Clyde. Well, I don't care what you say. I'm going to make up my own mind.

"We'll talk it over," said Gussie.

Then she went for a walk in the wind. She was worried about changing planes in that big, overwhelming Dallas airport, but she was also worried about Clyde's legs. His circulation was still bad, thanks to what that Fort Worth doctor had done to him so long ago. He also had back trouble from time to time, thanks to his old habit of picking up cars out of ditches. Ten hours in a car wouldn't be good for his legs or his back. She decided she couldn't do that to him. When she came back from her walk, Gussie announced that she would fly from Lubbock to Dallas alone. It was time to be brave. She could do it.

Clyde was disappointed, but he said all right, he'd put her on the plane in Lubbock. Get in. Let's go if we're going. Come on. Gussie thought they should call to make sure the planes were flying. Clyde said calling wouldn't do much good. Why? Because it took an hour and a half to get to the airport. What was true now might not be true when they got there. So off they went.

Clyde drove at fifty miles per hour—he was in no hurry—the seventy miles to the Lubbock airport. They went to the American Airlines ticket counter and learned that the flight had been canceled due to bad weather in Dallas.

Both Clyde and Gussie felt as if they had been granted a reprieve. They were glad the plane wasn't going. They loved the bad weather.

They went out to dinner at Chili's and then drove "home." The moon was out and shining brightly. They once again rolled down Route 40, the same way they had when she arrived. Soon there were two moons, one in the sky and the other shimmering on the surface of White River Lake. This was romance. The moon was big, their eyes were big, and they were in love. Not settle-for love. Not tired love. But real romantic love.

"What if," Clyde asked, "a coupla people who were never going to get married again, uh, uh—changed their minds?"

"Well, I don't know," said Gussie. "Do you know anybody like that?" She laughed.

"I expect maybe I do."

When they got back home, Clyde called a bald-headed doctor named Tom Bartholomew who lived in San Antonio. Tom was my best friend in high school. But why would my father be calling him? After all these years?

"Hello, Tom, how are you?" my father said. "This is Clyde Latham calling from Spur."

"I'm all right, Clyde," Tom said. "How're you?"

"I couldn't be better. I'm gonna get married again."

"You can't do that."

"Why not?"

"You're kids'll be younger"—Tom laughed—"than your grandkids."

"Well, frankly, unless we have an accident"—Clyde laughed too—"we don't plan to have a whole passel of kids."

"Oh, well, then that's all right."

Gussie stared at Clyde, surprised. He had mentioned the word "marriage" before, but always hypothetically, vaguely. He had certainly never proposed. Was this supposed to be a proposal? Was Clyde serious or just kidding? Could he be testing her? Trying to read her reaction? She decided to laugh—which could mean anything.

For Clyde, this phone call was a double test. He was watching to see how Gussie would react. But he was also listening for disapproval on the other end of the line. He was trying out this news on his son's high-school buddy before he tried it out on his son. His old heart stopped when Tom said: You can't do that! Would Aaron say the same? Or feel the same?

And we will sit upon the rocks, seeing the shepherds feed their flocks, by shallow rivers to whose falls . . .

22
The White Deer

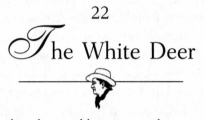

Come along, boys, and listen to my tale,
I'll tell you of my troubles on the old Chisholm trail.
Coma ti yi youpy, youpy ya, youpy ya,
Coma ti yi youpy, youpy ya.
—"The Old Chisholm Trail"

On a windy Tuesday, October 18, Clyde and Gussie started for the airport again. He reminded her that he had once traveled this road—the one between Spur and Lubbock—in a covered wagon. He pointed out the twin windmills, still standing, where he, his parents, and his brothers had camped one night. He was nine years old at the time.

His family was on the move because they were looking for a place where Glenn, the oldest of the Latham boys, wouldn't "up and die." He had tuberculosis of the bone—or so they said—and back then there was nothing that medicine could do for him. A doctor told the family that Glenn's only hope was to find a healthier climate, where he might improve. Hearing this news, Pop hitched up two horses to a covered wagon, and away they went. One horse was as black as a chuck-wagon frying pan, and the other had a white face, so they called one Blackie and the other Baldie. The Latham family headed west in their covered wagon as if the year were 1820 instead of 1920.

They rolled along a two-lane road, which they shared with automobiles and trucks. They were passed by Ford Model T's, the first Chevys, an occasional Cadillac with its brand-new V-8 engine, and very rarely a Stutz Bearcat, all rolling on solid rubber tires. Most had something in common with the covered wagon in their path: canvas tops.

On foot, the boys would get to playing and fall half a mile behind. Then they would have to run to catch the wagon again. They took turns riding an old white mare. Nights, the parents slept in a bed in the wagon while the boys slept under and around it.

"We had a chicken coop under the wagon to haul our chickens," Clyde told Gussie. "We let 'em out at night. One old rooster found a hen he liked and was trying to do some business with her. I went to jumping up and down and yelling, 'Whoopee, we'll have some eggs now!'" Clyde laughed warmly. "That's your nine-year-old, for you."

Gussie laughed, too.

The chickens weren't the only ones set free at night. The horses, Blackie and Baldie, were let out too, but their front feet were hobbled, tied together, so they wouldn't run off. They could still move about enough to graze, but they supposedly couldn't wander far.

"So one night, we camped at Two Windmills. We hobbled our horses as usual. We got up the next morning and there wasn't a horse in sight. And they always tell you that horses won't go back home. You take cows and dogs, and they'll go back toward home. But not horses. Anyway, Pop decided to look for them on the road home. A fellow in a Model T come along and picked him up. And eventually they caught up with them. Those horses had traveled eight miles—by the Model T's speedometer—with those hobbles on. Even jumped cattle guards. They'd started back home."

"Like me," Gussie said. "I guess I'm like a horse."

She expected him to laugh, but he didn't.

"Well, I'm takin' you back there," Clyde said in a hurt tone, "just as fast as I can."

"No, no, I didn't mean I was like a horse going home to California. I meant I was like a horse coming here. Back to my first home. I came back here—even though I never expected to—just like a dog or a cow or even an old horse."

"Well, you're sure nuff a pretty old horse," Clyde said, brightening.

The one-wagon wagon train had another setback a couple of days later. Pop was carrying his shotgun across his knees as he drove the team. He didn't notice when it slipped off and fell to the ground. When he finally realized that it was gone, he jumped on the white mare and rode back fourteen miles, until he finally found it. The wagon had run over the gun and broken its stock.

"Pop got out his pocketknife," Clyde told Gussie as they rolled along this familiar road, "and carved him a new one."

It took the covered wagon eight days to travel the 270 miles from Spur, Texas, to Carlsbad, New Mexico. They decided to stop and see if Glenn's health responded to the desert climate. Mom and Pop continued to sleep in the covered wagon, but now the boys had a small tent, where they bedded down on army cots.

They soon discovered wild burros in the area. The Latham boys spent many summer days catching those burros and riding them bareback. They also swam in the Pecos River. All but Glenn. He was still too sick.

After several months, Pop decided to move on to test another climate. This time they pinned their hopes on Hot Springs, New Mexico. Unfortunately, between Carlsbad and Hot Springs there was an obstacle: the Rocky Mountains. Pop didn't think they could make it in the covered wagon, so he bought a Model T truck.

They left on a Friday. The parents rode up front in the cab, the boys in the back. After they had gone only a few miles, the truck broke down.

"Pop said that he'd never start anything else on a Friday again," Clyde told Gussie.

Pop cranked and cranked, but the engine wouldn't start. Two cowboys rode up. One of them was an Englishman. Pop asked if they knew anything about trucks.

The Englishman said he did. He got down off his horse, pulled out the choke, and then cranked. Nothing. Cranked. Nothing. Cranked. Nothing at all. The Englishman got back on his horse and rode off without saying a word. Pop finally got the truck started without overseas aid.

As they climbed the Rockies, it started to snow. The

hard rubber tires spit and spun. The boys pushed, all but Glenn. They drove all day and covered only nineteen miles. They finally stopped at Cloudcroft, which was on top of a mountain. They spent the night in something called a "wagon yard," a precursor of the motel. There was shelter for horses and bare rooms for people. There were no beds. They all slept on the floor in bedrolls. There was a wood-burning stove, which they kept stoked all night so they wouldn't feeze to death.

The next day, they rolled down the other side of the mountain with bad brakes that just kept getting worse. Afraid they would go out completely, Pop started driving with two wheels on the road and the other two in the ditch to try to hold down the speed.

It took the Lathams six days to travel the 280 miles from Carlsbad to Hot Springs. They couldn't have done much worse in their old covered wagon.

"When we got to Hot Springs," Clyde told Gussie, "we all lived in a big tent. Mom put tow sacks on the earth floor and sprinkled them good to keep down the dust."

This tent was an army issue that was sixteen feet by sixteen feet with a center post that had a twelve-inch circumference. The mother and father slept in a brass bed—surrounded by the cots of their sons. When it rained, a stream ran through their home, passing right under the brass bed.

While they were at Hot Springs, Glenn bathed in the waters and was treated by a doctor with some original views. He told Pop to kill an albino deer and bring it to him. But where in the world would he find a white deer? Well, one had been seen lately down in the canyon. Pop got his gun and killed the snowy buck. The old doctor cooked up some kind of albino-deer stew and cured Glenn. Well, anyway, Glenn got better, whether it was the deer, the waters—or maybe he just got tired of being sick. (He had been told he would be dead by fourteen. He lived only until he was eighty-one.)

"When we finally come back home in 1924," Clyde told Gussie, "Dad traded the Model T truck for five horses. We come home in two covered wagons."

And we will sit upon the rocks, seeing the shepherds feed their flocks, by shallow rivers to whose falls melodious birds sing madrigals.

23
*O*ne Month

"And how long do you think we can keep up this goddamn coming and going?"

Florentino Ariza had kept his answer ready for fifty-three years, seven months, and eleven days and nights.

"Forever," he said.

—Gabriel García Márquez,
Love in the Time of Cholera

When Clyde and Gussie reached the Lubbock airport, at last, they found that her flight had once again been canceled. Flooding in Dallas. They went back to Chili's for dinner. On the ride home, the moon seemed even bigger. It was an omen, wasn't it? Gussie wasn't supposed to leave Spur. They were shuttling back and forth to the airport the way the old couple in *Love in the Time of Cholera* traveled up and down the same stretch of river "forever."

On these drives, back and forth, back and forth, they reviewed the lives they had lived away from each other, telling each other stories they already knew in part or in whole. They simply liked talking to each other.

"I was riding a plow back in 1931," Clyde said. "I come in at noon and this fellow told me to call R. E. Dixon, who was head of the experiment station."

This station was a glorified farm on the outskirts of Spur. There Texas A&M scientists ran all sorts of tests on all sorts of crops, but they specialized in cotton. Clyde called.

Dixon said: "Do you and your brother want to go to A&M?"

Clyde said: "No, sorry, we don't have any money."

Dixon said: "If you want to go, be here Saturday."

So eager were they, Clyde and his brother Abo showed up at the experiment station at dawn. Dixon told them they wouldn't be leaving until around four in the afternoon. He asked how much money they had.

Clyde said: "I've been plowing for a dollar a day for fifteen days."

Dixon said: "I'll give you sixteen more."

At a little after four in the afternoon, the boys piled into Dixon's car and they headed south.

They stopped in Abilene to eat dinner. Dixon did all the ordering: steak and potatoes for the boys, nothing for himself. When the steaks came, he asked the waitress for crackers and ketchup. While Clyde and Abo dug into their red-meat dinners, Dixon made a meal of saltines and the Heinz company's favorite sauce.

He said: "Let this be a lesson to you. If you don't have any money, you can still go ahead and eat."

In Abilene, Dixon put the boys on a train bound for College Station. When they arrived in Dallas, they got off to stretch their long legs and soon found themselves in the middle of a red-light district. The girls wanted the boys' money, but the brothers declined, explaining they had only thirty-one dollars between them and starvation. When they finally got to College Station, they had spent one dollar en route.

Clyde and Abo paid their way at A&M by playing basketball and working construction for the university. They carried radiators up four flights of stairs. They dug a steam tunnel four feet wide and eight feet deep. Then they went to basketball practice. Then they studied.

"It's a good thing that Aggie wanted you to call," Gussie said as they rolled along.

"I always thought so," said Clyde.

"Because I wouldn't be interested in you if you weren't a college man," she said.

He laughed.

"I'm serious," she said. "That's always been one of my requirements."

Then she laughed, too, but she meant what she said.

While Clyde was starting at Texas A&M, Gussie, three years younger, was going to dances in Kingman, Arizona, where she'd moved to be with her father.

"They'd have a couple of fiddles and a guitar and whatnot," Gussie told Clyde as they rolled on. "And it was good music to dance to because they played Texas music. And the women all brought cakes. And at midnight we had coffee and cakes."

"I sure do wish I'd been there," Clyde said.

"Me too. We'd have our refreshments at midnight, and then we'd dance on until the early morning. Until the sun came up. Or even later. Sometimes we'd keep right on dancing till noon."

In 1933, when she was twenty years old, Gussie married Charles Crismon, who manned an inspection station on the Arizona-California border: He was supposed to keep the likes of fruit flies out of the Grand Canyon state. In 1935, Gussie and Charles had a son, whom they named Fred after her father. The next year, 1936, Charles died of tuberculosis.

In 1939, Gussie married Bill Lancaster. Of course, that happened to be the same year that Clyde married Launa. Gussie's wedding was on Sunday, January 1st, in Winslow, Arizona. Then she spent her wedding night in a car driving from Kingman to Los Angeles.

"Bill had tickets for the Rose Bowl," Gussie explained. "Duke was playing USC."

The bridegroom—a USC Trojans fan—wasn't going to miss that game, marriage or no marriage. So on Monday, January 2nd, Gussie spent the first day of her honeymoon watching the University of Southern California beat Duke 7 to 3 in the world's largest honeymoon suite, a one-hundred-thousand-seat football stadium. At least it was named for a flower. So far as Bill was concerned, his marriage was off to a very good start. They won, didn't they?

Two years later, the Lancasters moved to Sacramento, where he worked for Beneficial Finance for almost forty years. Gussie and Bill had a daughter named Nola in 1944.

In 1964, Nola married an Air Force pilot, who flew for two years in Vietnam—he volunteered for the second year—and logged two hundred missions. Then he came home, started a flying school, and got killed taking off with a student pilot at the controls. They never made it over the trees.

In 1975, Nola married Tom Hall, an Air Force Top Gun turned airline pilot.

*O*n the third try, October 19th—after three Spur-to-Lubbock round-trips—the weather in Dallas finally improved. The planes were flying. Clyde waited with Gussie at the gate.

When Gussie's flight was announced, they kissed.

"I'll see you in about a month," Clyde said. "I'll come to California. Then maybe we'll talk some more about that couple who weren't ever going to get married again."

"Really?" said Gussie. "That would be nice."

"Yeah, in a month. That'll give that unmarrying couple some time to think things over. Where would they live? Texas or California? What would their kids think?"

"All right, a month. I'll see you in a month."

"Maybe."

Clyde and Gussie kissed again, this time longer, deeper, more hungrily. After all, this kiss was going to have to last them for a whole month.

Then Gussie got on the plane. Clyde just stood there, drained.

Now the waiting began. A month seemed like a very long time. But in a sense, Clyde had waited for Gussie for seventy years. He figured he could wait another thirty days.

And I will make you beds of roses . . .

24

$\mathscr{O}$ne Day

"I wouldn't ask too much of her," I ventured. "You can't repeat the past."

"Can't repeat the past?" he cried incredulously. "Why of course you can!"

—F. Scott Fitzgerald, *The Great Gatsby*

On my father's first day without Gussie, I called to see how he was doing. I was naturally afraid he might be depressed. I dialed his number and got a busy signal. I waited a few minutes and called again. It was still busy. I kept calling off and on for the next hour and a half. I was a little worried. Maybe he had knocked the phone off the hook attempting to call for help. I kept trying until finally:

"Hello."

"Hello, are you all right? Your phone's been busy—"

"Oh, I was just talkin' to Gussie."

I remembered the last time I had talked on the phone like that: It was when I was in high school.

Dad recounted for me a part of his long, long conversation with Gussie: He had told her that he'd kept his promise. He'd found himself a girlfriend. And her name was Gussie Lee.

"Could I talk to Lesley?" he asked.

"Sure," I said, a little surprised.

I handed her the phone.

"Hello," said Lesley.

"Hello, I've got an important question to ask you."

"All right."

"Do you think Aaron would be upset if I got married again?"

"No, absolutely not."

Lesley said it without hesitation and without checking with me. She knew that I was concerned about his being alone. Marriage would cure his loneliness and one of my main worries.

"In that case, I might just take a trip to California in the not too distant future."

"Good," said Lesley. "Go after her."

Lesley hung up and smiled at me. I returned her smile but with less voltage.

"Was that what it sounded like?" I asked.

"That's right," Lesley said. "He wanted to know if you would be upset if—"

"Well, will I?"

"No."

I shrugged. I shook my head. I was trying to get used to a second moon in the sky.

"Are you sure?" I asked.

"Of course," she said.

"How do you know, uh, I won't be—?"

"Upset? Because you're not an asshole. At least not last time I checked."

*C*lyde called Gussie back. She was surprised to hear from him again so soon. Gather you rosebuds.

"Will you pick me up at the airport tomorrow?" Clyde asked. "I'm coming to get you."

While you may.

Gussie was thrilled. She had made up her mind to wait for thirty days, but now she realized that even thirty hours would be much too long.

Old time is still a-flying.

The one-month waiting period had shrunk to one day. It was a great romantic gesture, a great romantic act. Clyde was in as much of a hurry as any teenager, maybe more. And Gussie was in a hurry too. Their old hearts raced.

And I will make you beds of roses and a thousand fragrant posies . . .

$\mathscr{U}$nbelievable

The maid is not dead, but sleepeth.
—Matthew 9:24

I woke up in the night and couldn't go back to sleep. I got up and wandered downstairs. I found myself staring out the window at the roof of the Museum of Natural History. In the silver light, it looked even more like a castle than usual. I found some comfort in its seeming permanence, immutability, solidness.

Staring down on Natural History, I started musing ironically about animals that mate for life. The miniature African antelope called the dik-dik. Snow geese. Coyotes. I wondered: What did they do if their life's mate died or got killed or was eaten? Did they remain faithful forever? Or did the widows and widowers ever pair up again? Were there dik-dik stepmothers? Somehow I couldn't imagine it. Was my father less loyal than a rabbit-sized antelope? Or was I just being a dick?

I went into the kitchen to get a drink of grapefruit

juice. I drank from the carton and sat down at the kitchen table. I remembered standing in the doorway of my mother's hospital room. Then setting down my suitcase and computer, I started across the room to wake her up. I was surprised that my father wasn't around. He was *always* there. Maybe he had gone down to get something to eat. My mother was more jaundiced than I had ever seen her. It hurt to find her so yellow. Her mouth was slightly open. Her teeth looked smaller than I remembered and appeared jagged. I was reaching out to shake her shoulder when I heard my wife calling from behind me.

"Aaron, we're too late!" Lesley said in a strained voice. "Aaron! Aaron!"

I stopped short, frightened, and stared at my mother. She didn't look dead. She looked as if she were about to open her eyes and talk to me. I could almost hear the familiar voice. I just couldn't believe it. Dead? No. My mother? No. She was the floor under my whole life. That floor couldn't collapse. What would I stand on?

What was I standing on?

I still couldn't believe that she was dead at her funeral. Maybe that's why I didn't cry. It wasn't real. We were all there under a false premise. I didn't cry at the cemetery either. I was miserable, numb, hurt, but dry-faced in the West Texas wind. To cry would mean that it was all real.

My father cried.

And now he was about to remarry. It almost seemed bigamy to me. As if he would have two living wives. I still could not believe she was gone.

I got up, put the grapefruit juice back in the refrigerator, and climbed back up to bed. I would try to sleep, but sleeping was a little too much like dying for my current mood.

And I will make you beds of roses and a thousand fragrant posies, a cap of flowers, and a kirtle . . .

26

$\mathcal{I}$ Love You!!!

Ah, when to the heart of man
     Was it ever less than a treason
To go with the drift of things,
     To yield with a grace to reason,
And bow and accept the end
     Of a love or a season?
       —Robert Frost, "Reluctance"

The next day when I called my father, the phone wasn't busy, but nobody answered. My dad had flown to Sacramento to tell Gussie he couldn't wait any longer.

"Gussie, I want to get married right now," Clyde said upon his arrival. "I don't want to wait. Will you marry me right now?"

But at my back I always hear, time's banged-up old buggy rattling near.

"I'll marry you," she said, "but I won't live in your house. It's too big. I don't want us to spend the rest of our lives trying to keep it up."

Of course, hearing the story later, nobody believed

that she didn't want to live in the house because it was too big. Everybody thought she didn't want to live there because it was my mother's house. But everybody was sympathetic.

"That's fine," Clyde said. "We'll buy a place."

"Okay, we'll get married then."

"Right now?"

"Right now!"

So they were engaged.

When Gussie was younger, getting engaged didn't necessarily mean getting married, not to her it didn't. She was once engaged to five men at the same time. But now she was older and surer. At eighty-one, one engagement would do just fine, thank you. Preferably a short one. Very short.

Now it was time for Clyde to meet his future stepchildren. They started with Gussie's son, Fred, sixty, who lived in San Jose. He turned out to be tall and handsome with thick, iron-gray hair. He and his wife, Dorothy, who looked a lot like him, invited the engaged couple to spend a few days in their modest suburban home. The house was filled with Fred's abstract paintings, which had always puzzled his mother.

Soon Gussie's daughter, Nola, who looked like Goldie Hawn, came rolling up the driveway. This fifty-year-old had in tow her pretty, blond, seventeen-year-old daughter, Colleen, who wasn't happy. This teenager didn't think that her octogenarian grandmother should get married again. Love was for the young.

Later that evening she overheard Clyde and Gussie having what they thought was a private conversation.

Colleen couldn't help eavesdropping because the old folks were talking so loud: They had taken out their hearing aids.

"I'M SO HAPPY," yelled her grandmother. "I LOVE YOU, CLYDE."

"I LOVE YOU, TOO, GUSSIE," Clyde shouted back.

Colleen changed her mind about her grandma getting married. Gussie was clearly in love and more or less shouting it from the rooftops.

𝒞lyde and Gussie wasted no time setting a date. They would get married on November 1—just one short week after my dad's arrival in California. And they would elope. They had talked about taking more time and planning a larger wedding, but they decided they just couldn't wait. They found a minister in Santa Cruz who could marry them on a Tuesday morning at 11:00, but they had to be out of the church by 11:45. This was a busy preacher. She was booked.

The night before it the happy couple was still in residence in San Jose. This was an appropriate launching pad for Clyde and Gussie's never-too-late marriage, for Fred and Dorothy had gotten married, both for the first time, when they were both forty-seven years old. And it had worked for them.

On his wedding eve, my dad was sitting on the bed in the guest bedroom when he heard laughter. He looked up and there were Fred and Dorothy laughing at him.

Embarrassed, self-conscious, the bridegroom asked: "What's so funny?"

Dorothy said: "Your pajamas match the sheets."

Clyde looked. His blue-striped pajamas did indeed match the blue-striped sheets. Now he laughed too.

And I will make you beds of roses and a thousand fragrant posies, a cap of flowers, and a kirtle embroidered all with leaves of myrtle.

27

*H*ow Long Have You Been Married?

Let us, like burrs, together stick.
—John Gay,
"A New Song
of New Similes"

The bride and groom got up early and dressed in their wedding clothes. He wore a light-brown leather sports coat over a dark brown shirt with tan pants. He topped all this off with a black bolo tie. She wore a black skirt with a matching black turtleneck. She added another layer with a red cardigan sweater, which she buttoned in front.

Getting up early had been Fred's idea. He wanted to swing by the church before breakfast so they would be sure they knew how to find it. With only a forty-five-minute window of opportunity, they couldn't afford to get lost and be late. They were all hungry when they got in Fred's car and headed toward Santa Cruz.

They found the church without much trouble and then drove down to the ocean. They picked out a nice café on the wharf, filed inside, and ordered: eggs, bacon, and croissants. When Fred told the waiter that they were a wedding party, the octogenarian bride blushed and the octogenarian groom beamed. Soon the other waiters and even other customers were coming by to offer best wishes and congratulations. The sea lions in the harbor joined in with happy yelps. After breakfast, as they were leaving, the bride and groom got another round of felicitations, only this time the voices were louder.

"BEST WISHES!"

"CONGRATULATIONS!"

"BE HAPPY!"

They all climbed back into Fred's car and headed for the church, but somehow they got lost. Getting up so early, leaving the house hungry, had all been for nought. Soon Fred and Dorothy were fighting.

"Go this way."

"No, it's that way."

And everybody was checking his or her watch.

"Let's stop and ask directions."

"No, we can find it."

Naturally, it was Dorothy who wanted to stop for directions, and it was Fred who didn't. All marriages seem to take on this configuration. Did this conjugal quarrel cause the bride and groom to have any second thoughts about the chances for conjugal bliss?

"We're going to be late!"

"I'm doing the best I can."

"No, you're not, not if you won't stop and ask."

"Stopping would just waste time."

"It's eleven. We're already late."

"There it is!"

The bride and groom arrived at the church for their wedding just as the preacher was getting out of her car. Then another car pulled up with Gussie's daughter, Nola, and her granddaughter, Colleen, inside. They presented the bride with a bouquet of roses. They were yellow, as in "The Yellow Rose of Texas." And they were tied with a ribbon that was yellow, too, as in *She Wore a Yellow Ribbon*.

Fred had brought along a present, too, but he wouldn't say what it was. The gift was wrapped in a large box. Fred carried it into the church and set it down in the first pew that he came to. Gussie tried to kid her son into giving away his secret, but he stood mute. His mom would just have to wait and be surprised.

The preacher greeted them. She was a short woman with dark brown hair going gray at the temples. She wore gray slacks, a turquoise blouse, and a constant smile.

The church organist arrived to do some paperwork. When she discovered a wedding about to get under way, she volunteered to play and sing for the ceremony. This happy coincidence gave the bride and groom a sense of fate, of doing the right thing, of it was meant to be.

At the beginning of the service, the organist played and sang "The First Time Ever I Saw Your Face." It was her choice, but an apt one. They had first seen each other's faces fourscore years ago. Clyde whispered to

Gussie: "Remember, I've loved you since you were three years old."

"Marriage is a sacred promise," intoned the preacher, "a promise to love each other with tenderness and forgiveness; to honor and respect each other's need to be an individual as well as a couple; to cherish each moment you share, whether of laughter or tears, pleasure or pain; to protect the flame of love which unites you now; and to remember to love one another as you are, not as you think you should be, or even could be."

The bride stood there beside her groom thinking: Teenagers don't have a monopoly on love. She was sure she hadn't felt any more deeply when she was just a girl. And she had never thought she would ever feel this way again, not at her age, not when she was already older than she had ever imagined being. It was a miracle, just a miracle.

"This is my prayer for you," the preacher continued. "May you always need one another, seek one another, want one another, encourage one another, and embrace one another and so doing discover the love that expands, enfolds, embraces all."

Nola, Dorothy, and Colleen were all crying, but crybaby Gussie didn't shed any tears. She was too happy, too transported, too dreamy, in some sort of trance.

"Finally, give each other your loving attention, your understanding, your laughter and playfulness, your protection and support, day in and day out, for better or for worse, for richer or for poorer, in sickness and in health, for as long as you both shall live."

They were both nodding.

"Do you, Clyde, take Gussie to be your wedded wife, to

love her, respect her, provide for her, and be to her a devoted husband?"

"I do."

"Do you, Gussie, take Clyde to be your wedded husband, to love him, respect him, provide for him, and be to him a devoted wife?"

"I do."

After the ceremony, Fred fetched the big box from the back of the church. Clyde and Gussie opened it and discovered lots of cowboy hats. Fred handed them out. He gave his mother a black felt hat, which happened to match her skirt and sweater. Clyde got another black hat. Nola got a blue one. Colleen a tan one. Dorothy's was tan, too. Fred gave himself a white hat. Was there some oedipal echo in this choice of hats, a black hat for his new stepfather, a white one for himself? Probably not. Standing in front of the altar, they all posed for pictures in their new cowboy hats.

Then they adjourned to a Mexican restaurant, where they had enchiladas, tacos, refried beans, and margaritas. It was the first time Clyde had had a drink in twenty-five years. He just never smoked or drank—no big deal—but he was willing to make an exception on his wedding day.

Soon the wedding party was on the road again. Now the bride and groom rode with Nola and Colleen. They snaked their way up and down narrow, winding mountain roads. They passed through the small town of Boulder Creek and then pulled up in front of a spectacular redwood house. Nola and Colleen were home. They ushered the newlyweds inside.

Then Nola and Colleen announced that they had some

shopping to do. They obviously wanted to give the bride and groom some time alone. Clyde sat down in a big easy chair in the redwood living room. Gussie sat in his lap. They kissed. And that is how Nola and Colleen found them when they came back from shopping.

Then the newlyweds called New York. Lesley, Taylor, and I were all stunned, not that they had gotten married, but that they had gotten married so soon. I hadn't even met my new stepmother and didn't really know how I felt about her. I tried to say the right things.

"Congratulations. . . . Best wishes. . . . Good luck. . . . Hope you're old enough to know what you're doing."

That night, Gussie and Clyde closed the guest-room door and went to bed together for the first time, as husband and wife. They hugged. They kissed passionately again and again. And that was enough for the first night of their conjugal life. But they were both thinking: Perhaps we'll try more on some other night. They went to sleep in each other's arms.

A few days later, Clyde and Gussie flew home to Spur. While they were in the air, they chattered away about the relatives, about each other, about their adventure to come, about just about everything. My father remembers: "Both of us just talked as hard as we could." It seemed a short flight.

When they landed in Lubbock, a total stranger approached them and said: "It's great that you two still find each other so interesting. You talked the whole way. Tell me: How long have you two been married?"

Gussie said: "Three days."

The stranger's expression collapsed.

When the honeymooners reached Spur, the preacher's wife said: "No more live-ins. I want to see your marriage license."

A gown made of the finest wool . . .

28
O Pioneers

Then together in double harness
They will trot along down the line,
Until death shall call them over
To a bright and sunny clime.

May your joys be then completed
And your sorrows have amend,
Is the fondest wish of the writer,—
Your true and faithful friend.
                              —"Dan Taylor"

After packing hurriedly, my wife and I raced to a wedding reception that was to take place at the Pitchfork Ranch. This ranch had helped Clyde woo Gussie, and now it would help him celebrate his triumph. So it would be at the Pitchfork that I would first meet the woman my father had married: my new stepmother.

On the way to the party at the Pitchfork, Lesley and I had airline troubles. We got stuck in Dallas for hours. This delay gave me even more time to wonder and worry about my father's new wife. Not only had I never met her, but I didn't remember ever having seen a photograph of her. All I knew was that she was one of the Willis girls. I kept thinking: It's unusual not to know your own stepmother. And I worried: What if the marriage didn't work? What if it was all a mistake? What if they really had been in too much of a hurry? I understood why they had hurried, but still . . .

When we finally arrived at the historic ranch, we passed under a Pitchfork brand that was three feet tall. We wound down a dirt road shaded by cottonwoods, then pulled into a circular drive in front of ranch headquarters. It was a large white house with four columns in front and four gables on top. A cowboy Tara.

Lesley and I climbed stiffly out of the rented car. On the way to the front door, we were intercepted by my favorite cousin, Lynn Latham, who was smiling.

"It's really love," she said. "They can't keep their hands off each other."

I smiled and shrugged.

Inside, my father introduced us to his bride. This eighty-one-year-old looked like a sixty-year-old. A pretty sixty-year-old. I was really quite surprised at how handsome she was. But it wasn't how *she* looked that most surprised me. Almost shocked me. It was how my father looked. He beamed. He radiated happiness, goodwill, contentment, pride, joy. He had never looked all that old, but he looked younger now. Gussie completed him, elevated him, energized him, made his eyes dance, made his lips twitch into smile after smile. They leaned against each other. His arm was around her.

Was my cousin right? Was it real love? Or was it infatuation? Could these octogenarians be locked in some sort of physical fascination that would cool with time? Was I crazy? What was wrong with me? Why couldn't I just relax and enjoy the party?

I kept remembering how many times Gussie had made promises to my father and then disappointed him. Could it happen again? How long would she last in this hard country? Originally she hadn't wanted to come. Now that she was here, did she really want to stay?

It seemed that most of the town of Spur was crowded into the big living room under the thirteen-foot ceiling. The space was dominated by a large oil painting of a roundup: ten mounted cowboys, a chuck wagon, and a dark sky with rain—good news in these parts—falling in the distance. This picture by the western artist Gary Niblett hung over a large fireplace, which was equipped with antler-handled andirons. Overhead the massive chandelier was made of deer antlers too. Two overstuffed easy chairs were upholstered with material cut from Indian blankets. On the floor was an Indian rug. The house, which dated back a hundred years, was even older than the guests of honor.

A fellow and his wife turned up. They were total strangers who had heard about the party and had invited themselves. They were welcomed in that great western tradition of y'all come. The couple said they would like to sing some songs in honor of the newlyweds. Well, the more the merrier, especially if they volunteered to entertain. The bride and groom couldn't help remembering the church organist who just turned up by accident on the morning of their wedding. Here was another coincidence that felt like fate, like some kind of blessing. The musical couple sang the old songs:

For your wedding supper, there'll be beef and cornbread;
There it is to eat when the ceremony's said,
And when you go to milk you'll milk into a gourd;
And set it in the corner and cover it with a board;
Some gets a little and some gets none,
For that is the way of the Texians,
For that is the way of the Texians.

I was getting more and more nervous because I knew I should make a toast. Talking to crowds scares me. Addressing more than one person at a time scares me. And sometimes one is too many. I had been trying to compose something on the plane. Naturally, I wasn't going to mention my reservations. Quite the contrary. I would make the most optimistic speech possible—as if saying it would make it so. I finally decided I couldn't put it off any longer.

"We are happy to be here today"—my heart was thumping irregularly, or so it seemed—"because Clyde and Gussie give us all hope. These newlyweds are going ahead of us, holding up romantic torches to light our way to love, to falling in love, to being in love at any age. They're from pioneer stock and they're still pioneers marking the trail."

A gown made of the finest wool which from our pretty lambs we pull . . .

29

Granny

I remember, I remember,
The house where I was born.
—Thomas Hood,
  "I Remember, I Remember"

After the party at the Pitchfork, we drove back to the home where the woman of the house had always been my mother. Would I resent Gussie's presence there? Would I find her out of place among all of Mom's things, the landscapes she had painted hanging on the walls, the children's books she had written on the shelf?

When the four of us—Gussie, Clyde, Lesley, and I—sat down at an elaborately carved dining table surrounded by my mother's dishes, I tried hard to dislike my stepmother. But it was difficult. She was so cheerful, so open, so happy. And she obviously made my father happy, too. At least today. Before anything went wrong. Before anything bad happened. I could see that my dad loved Gussie—which made me love her and not love her at the same time. I loved her out of loyalty to my father, but I didn't love her out of loyalty to my mom.

"How did you two first meet?" asked Lesley.

"You mean way back when?" asked Clyde. "Well, we've known each other forever."

"As Clyde always says," Gussie said, "we were born in the same house."

"Clyde never said that to me," I said. "Why were you born in the same house? Was there some house shortage back then?"

"No," my father said, "there were lots more houses back then than there are now."

"Was it the doctor's house?" asked Lesley.

"No, the doctor made house calls," Gussie said. "That was the old days."

"Whose house was it?" I wanted to know. "What's going on? Is this some kind of secret or something?"

The newlyweds exchanged a conspiratorial look.

"Or something," Clyde said.

My father and his bride told the story together: That house—the one where they were both born—belonged to a woman whose maiden name was Frances Willis. She came to Texas to escape a deadly feud being fought out in Arkansas. Several members of her family had already been killed, and she had had enough. She had no way of knowing that West Texas would be every bit as bloody as Arkansas.

She married a man named Goodall and they bought a ranch ten miles east of the town of Spur. This land had been part of the old Spur Ranch, which was then being broken up and sold off. Her husband became a judge in this often lawless country. Judge and Mrs. Goodall had six children: Rob, Sally Harriet (who hated her name), Effie, Willie, Joe, and Joe's twin brother, who was born dead.

Then one night—back when Spur was still a rough cowtown—this Judge Goodall got killed coming home from the saloon. He had gotten in an argument at the bar that ended in an old-fashioned gunfight. It was like a western movie, but the dead stayed dead.

The widow Goodall stayed on in Spur for some time and then disappeared to Arkansas. When she returned a year later, she brought with her a mysterious baby boy, whom she called Fred Willis. He was first explained as an orphan whom she had adopted. Later on, he was explained as her sister's boy. But Spur didn't believe these explanations. Nonetheless, Mrs. Goodall always maintained that she was doing the Lord's work by taking him in.

Eventually, Mrs. Goodall married a Mr. Adams and became Mrs. Goodall-Adams. Once again, she started having children. Of course, these—Olvie, Gen, John, and Hool—had the last name of Adams. So there were the Goodall kids . . . the Willis boy . . . and then the Adams kids . . . ten children in all.

All too soon, Mr. Adams went the way of Mr. Goodall. He was murdered in another gunfight coming home from the Spur saloon. Then Granny Goodall-Adams, twice widowed, lost her favorite son. Her boy Joe Goodall got his foot hung up in a stirrup and his horse dragged him to death. That happened over at Duck Creek while he was still just a teenager. Then John got shot dead. Granny had lost two husbands and two sons to violence of one kind or another in this wild place. Her people just kept on dying too soon.

One of the Goodall children, the girl with the hated name Sally Harriet, grew up and married a boy named John Henry Latham. And they had six strapping boys: Glenn, Joe, Clyde (Dub), Albert (Abo), John (Mutt), and Francis (Chick) the baby. The Latham boys.

Meanwhile, the mysterious Willis boy grew up and married Annie Eva Boothe. Fred and Annie had four girls: The Willis girls. Orree, Gussie, Frances, and Pauline. The four Willis girls grew up with the six Latham boys. Neither the boys nor the girls were told that they might be related. But Annie, the mother of the Willis girls, told her daughters over and over again: "Never marry a Latham." Which only made the Latham boys more interesting to the Willis girls.

"So that's why we were born in the same house," Gussie said. "We both had the same grandmother. Granny Goodall-Adams. And she had a big house."

Lesley and I looked at each other. My God. Here was a family secret I had never heard a whisper of. Here was a rich interlocking past I hadn't even imagined. Our family's history had twists and turns that were both intriguing and disturbing. I couldn't help wondering: Why hadn't I known? Had I not been curious enough? Or had others been too secretive? Now that I knew, my great-grandmother was promoted from ignored ancestor to mythic figure.

Lesley's reaction was more straightforward: "You can't get married. You're cousins. You're going to have to get an annulment." She was smiling.

"Well, we're not plannin'"—my father was grinning broadly—"to have a housefulla kids."

"That's right," said Gussie. "We promise."

Then my dad looked serious. "One day, Abo and I'd been down in the breaks, and when we come in, Mom was standing in the door with a razor strap. We said: What are you going to do, Mom? She said: I'm going to beat you kids to death. We said: Why? She said: You've been talking about the Willis girls. We said: Noooo!!! We haven't!"

"What did she do?" I asked.

"She finally hung the strap back up," Clyde said. "I expect somebody said something about the Willis girls. About Gran and so forth. About all that mix-up. All that old gossip. And it got back to Mom, and she thought we were behind it, and she was just gonna beat us to death. That's all."

"Your mother was the only one who really loved us," Gussie told Clyde.

A gown made of the finest wool which from our pretty lambs we pull; fair lined slippers for the cold . . .

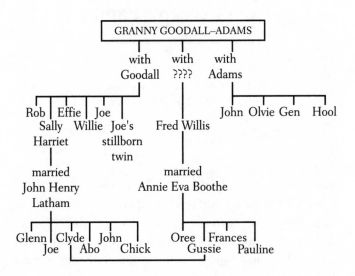

30

A Weepy Family

'Twas Christmas told the merriest tale.
—Sir Walter Scott, *Marmion*

We planned a big Christmas. The newlyweds caught a plane for California. My wife, my daughter, and I flew in from New York. Nola and Tom's older daughter, Annie, and her husband, Scott, a marine, drove up from San Diego. And they brought along a marine buddy named Ray, so Scott would have somebody to play soldier with. We all gathered in the big redwood house in Boulder Creek for the holidays. Gussie and Clyde. Taylor, Lesley, and me. Tom, Nola, and Colleen. Annie, Scott, and Ray. Fred and Dorothy. And Tom's ninety-year-old mother, Helen.

It was an old-fashioned, big-family Christmas, with the focus not on the children, as usually happens, but rather on an eighty-four-year-old and an eighty-one-year-old. Gussie kept saying that she had never gotten so many presents. Growing up an orphan, more or less, she had been passed over on many Christmas mornings. Now she cried. But then so did her granddaughter Colleen, her daughter, Nola, and her son-in-law, Tom. Clyde had married into a weepy family.

Halfway through opening the presents, a family of deer—a buck and three does—emerged from the redwoods and started eating the backyard. Seeing deer always makes you happy.

Of course, everybody wanted to know all about the newlyweds' new marriage. They responded by telling stories. Gussie told about the time her bridegroom wanted to party.

"He called me 'Honey Bun,'" she said, "and wanted to know what I thought about stopping at the liquor store. I said, 'Honey Bun?' And he said, 'That's right, how about it?'"

Gussie was surprised that her new husband wanted to stop at a liquor store because he didn't drink. They had been out driving, just appreciating the scenery. Some might not agree that there was any such thing as scenery around Spur, but they haven't looked long enough or hard enough.

"Clyde said he wanted to pick up some apricot brandy and celebrate. I asked, 'Celebrate what?' He said, 'Well, it's a pretty old world.' So that's what we were going to celebrate."

They stopped at Tip's liquor store in Dickens. They couldn't shop for alcohol in Spur because the town is dry. So they drove the ten miles to Dickens and bought a pint of apricot brandy.

Then they drove "home." They were still living in the

old house where my father had lived with my mother. They were looking for a new place to call home, but so far they hadn't found anything.

Clyde and Gussie sat in the side-by-side recliners where he had first told her that he loved her and the world had lurched on its axis. They talked and talked and sipped apricot brandy out of champagne glasses. Seeing her husband's glass empty, Gussie refilled it. Then her own. Then his again. They discussed how happy they were and how lucky they were. And they kept toasting each other until the bottle was empty.

The next morning, Gussie got up and started fixing breakfast. Clyde stayed in bed, which was unusual for him. He was normally an early riser. She went back into the bedroom to check on him.

"He told me his head hurt," Gussie said with a big smile. "He thought he had a virus. But I set him straight. I told him that he didn't have a virus at all. I informed him that he had a hangover."

She gave him three tablespoons of Pepto-Bismol. He went back to sleep and slept for five hours. When he woke up, he was fine.

When his bride finished her story, Clyde told us all: "Drinkin's over-rated. Only took me eighty-four years to find that out."

The weepy family laughed until it cried.

*A*t the dinner table that evening, Gussie said: "I just knew I wasn't going to get married again. Not at my advanced age. I didn't think about falling in love again. When you get to be eighty-one, you don't think of love."

Clyde interrupted in a loud voice: "Oh, yes you do!!"
Gussie blushed.

A gown made of the finest wool which from our pretty
lambs we pull; fair lined slippers for the cold, with buckles
of the purest gold.

31

The Marriage Bed

Love and a cottage!
—George Colman,
The Clandestine Marriage

Shortly after they got back to Spur, Clyde and Gussie received an unexpected call.

"We've solved your problem," said a familiar voice. "We've found you a place to live."

"What?" asked Clyde.

"Where?" asked Gussie.

"With us."

D'Ann and Robert Pierce were at the other end of the line. He is an executive with the Spur Security Bank. She works at the bank, too. She has the features of the blond prom queen she once was, but now, after two children, she is always fighting her weight. Robert has a round face and looks to be an overgrown child. Neither husband nor wife looks like a banker. Like Gussie, Robert grew up an orphan. When he heard that Clyde and

Gussie were looking for a new place to live, he wanted to help out.

Robert and D'Ann told Clyde and Gussie that they could live in a guest house on their ranch. It would cost them a dollar a year. The four of them went out to take a look. They drove two miles outside of Spur city limits, turned right at a lone mailbox, crossed a bumpy cattleguard, then followed a dirt road lined with tall elm trees that were almost as old as the newlyweds. They soon came to a fork in the road: The left fork led to a big, handsome, steep-roofed, red-brick ranch house, while the right fork wound its way to the guest house, built of matching red brick with white trim. The two homes looked like Papa Bear and Baby Bear. Gussie and Clyde were thrilled and thankful. It was certainly a pretty old world.

Soon they were packing and moving. This event developed into an old-fashioned barn-raising as lots of neighbors showed up to lend a hand. Spur High School football players did most of the heavy lifting. A friend named Benny Ball turned up with a pickup and a fifteen-foot trailer. A father-and-son team, Junior Day and thirteen-year-old Travis, arrived with tools and know-how and built a front porch. Mike Day, Junior's cousin, brought along his nine-year-old daughter, Wendy; they got busy hooking up the washer, drier, and dishwasher. A Texas Tech student named Mitch Calhoun who was studying interior decoration dropped by to help arrange the furniture and hang pictures on the walls. D'Ann Pierce and her children, Emily, nine, and Mason, seven, baked cookies and put paper on all the shelves. A bookcase wouldn't fit through the door, so Clyde sawed it in half—as if he were a magician and it were a lady.

While all this hard work was going on, a longhorn steer watched curiously from the other side of a barbed-wire fence. He was reddish brown with a few white spots on his flanks and a classic rack of horns. Occasionally he flicked away a fly with his tail. This relic of Texas history belonged to the ranch next door and would be the newlyweds' closest neighbor.

At the end of the day, Gussie was "so tired she couldn't wiggle." Clyde wasn't wiggling much either. They were so exhausted they couldn't wait to get to bed—for the first time in their new home!—but the bed wasn't made up. They went into the master bedroom and discovered that one of the bed frame's casters was missing. It was on Clyde's side, which was of course the heavy side. The bed rocked.

Giving up on the bedroom, the newlyweds moved into the living room. They unfolded the couch, which turned into a queen-sized bed. Ah, now! But they couldn't find any queen-sized sheets. So they folded up the couch again—a job in itself—and returned oh so wearily to the bedroom.

Gussie finally found the missing caster and used a Kleenex to wedge it into its socket. Now maybe it wouldn't come out again, anyway not until the next morning. Two hours after they had started trying to turn in for the night, the newlyweds finally fell into their unsteady marriage bed. The bed might be wobbly, but the marriage didn't seem to be. New love in old bottles. Old eyes seeing new horizons. A new beginning in an old land. Yes, hope for us all.

Too sentimental? Well, maybe, but why not call a spade a spade? Or in this case, a heart a heart?

Gussie and Clyde slept well that night.

A belt of straw and ivy buds . . .

32
*S*ex

Kiss till the cows come home.
—Francis Beaumont and
John Fletcher, *Scornful Lady*

The next morning, they found cows grazing on their front yard and backyard. They were a handsome French breed called Limousins, tall and roan-colored. These curiously named cows not only invaded the yard but also got into the newlyweds' garage. They left cow chips on the sidewalk. They even climbed up on their new porch. The Limousins sometimes frightened Gussie, who hadn't lived in cow country for almost seventy years. Soon the cows were having calves. It was springtime.

"Gussie, we could use your help tomorrow," Robert Pierce said. "How about it?"

"Sure, anything," she said. "What?"

"Well, we're gonna be doin' a little artificial insemination. Need all the hands we can get."

"What would my job be?"

"Oh, I dunno, maybe sticking your arm three feet up a cow's vagina."

"Robert!"

*J*ust as Gussie was shy about entering a cow, I was shy about entering upon the subject of octogenarian love-making. I just couldn't imagine asking my father: How's your sex life? Do you *sleep* with your wife? But I wanted to know the answer to these questions for several reasons: Because I wondered if it was a "real marriage." Because I wanted to know what to expect in my own life. And because I wanted to write about this honeymoon couple. But how do you ask your father about his sex life? I called my dad every night, and every night I planned to ask him, but . . .

While I was still trying to decide how to broach this subject, I happened to cross the path of Helen Gurley Brown, the author of *Sex and the Single Girl* and the editor of *Cosmopolitan* magazine. We were seated next to each other at a dinner party. I confessed to her my problem.

"I can tell you what they do," Helen said. "They touch each other. It's easier for her because she's a woman. He doesn't get fully erect, but he enjoys it anyway. Talk to Gussie. It'll be easier for her to talk about it."

Taking Helen's advice, I called. My father answered. I asked for Gussie. He put her on. I confessed that I couldn't ask my father a certain question but that I was prepared to ask her. Please sit down. Then I asked if she and my father had a sex life. The Atlantic Ocean—my blood—roared in my ears.

"My sex life has always been very private," Gussie said. "But I can tell you that we have love and respect, hugging and kissing."

"Good news," I said.

"Younger people think they have all the sex feelings, but older people have them, too. It's not like when you're young, but you still have the drive. You still like to be touched. You have the same desire."

She paused, embarrassed. Since I was embarrassed myself, I didn't say anything either.

"Here, talk to your father," she said at last.

Which was just what I had hoped to avoid!

"We've been wonderin'," my dad said, "when you were gonna get around to askin' about that."

"Oh, really?"

"Well, when you get older, you still have all the feelings you had when you were young," said my dad. "Women can still do everything, anything. But men can't do like women. Sometimes they can't get all the way up, but it's still good. Makes you feel great."

At their age, making love was no longer goal oriented. It wasn't about scoring. It wasn't about procreation. It wasn't even necessarily about orgasm. My father, the coach, told me that in your eighties, making love wasn't anymore about winning or losing: It really was about how you played the game. And playing that game was still fun.

Father and son had finally had their first talk about sex.

Gussie wanted the phone back.

"When I'm in love," she said, "I have these feelings. I've never had them unless I was very deeply in love."

A belt of straw and ivy buds, with coral clasps and amber studs . . .

33

In Sickness and in Health

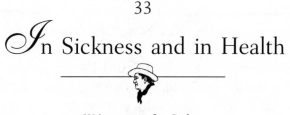

We're waiting for Godot.
—Samuel Beckett

Gussie and Clyde had a new house and a new marriage. They were feeling happy and lucky when overnight their luck changed. It was the day before Easter. Clyde woke up in the night with his left foot throbbing. It hurt so bad he could hardly stand it. Gussie drove her husband to the nearest hospital, which was thirty-five miles away, in Crosbyton. They were met by Dr. Kirk Chandler, my father's longtime doctor and friend, who elevated the painful foot and prescribed blood thinners. Knowing my father's medical history, the doctor naturally suspected a circulation problem.

"Gussie, don't look so serious," Clyde said.

"I'm worried about you, honey."

"Don't worry about me. I don't worry about you. Worry gives you wrinkles."

Gussie laughed, and her serious expression softened slightly.

The honeymoon couple spent Easter Sunday in the hospital. They held hands. They kissed.

"I wish we had more privacy," Clyde whispered to Gussie.

They both laughed.

The next day, they went home. Clyde's foot was fine for the first couple of days, but then it started hurting again. Needing help, Gussie called D'Ann. They managed to get Clyde into a borrowed pickup. Then they drove the thirty-five miles back to the Crosbyton hospital.

Dr. Chandler examined Clyde's foot and then ran more tests. My father was in physical and mental pain.

"I'm worried about Gussie," Clyde told Dr. Chandler over and over. "It's not fair to her. I didn't mean to get her into all this."

For better or for worse, in sickness and in health . . . but he had never imagined that this clause of the marriage contract would be tested so soon. He felt guilty and a little uneasy about Gussie. Was she feeling cheated? Trapped?

Growing more and more concerned about my father's foot, Dr. Chandler suggested moving Clyde to St. Mary's Hospital in Lubbock, which was another thirty-five miles away. This time the patient went by ambulance.

In Lubbock, doctors ran test after test on my father. They quickly discovered that poor circulation was indeed the problem: Clyde was still paying for medical mistakes made half a century earlier. In fact, the doctors couldn't detect a pulse in his left foot at all, probably because blood clots were clogging the veins and arteries. These clots were a special concern because one might dislodge itself and make its way to his brain, which could cause a stroke, or to his heart, which could set off a coronary.

Dr. Fawwaz Shoukfeh, a heart specialist who had treated my father before, announced that he would operate in the morning. He planned to place screens in both legs. These screens would keep the dangerous clots at home in the lower extremities—far away from my father's heart and brain. They would act something like gutter gratings that keep large objects out of the sewer. My father took the news stoically, as he had some thirty other times in his life when he faced surgery.

"Remember that albino buck I told you about?" asked Clyde.

"Of course," said Gussie.

"Kinda wish another one of them white deer would turn up."

Worrying about the surgery to come in the morning, Gussie went home that night to pack a bag. She would return early the next day with enough changes of clothing to stay for many days and nights. She slept poorly.

The next morning at 5 A.M., D'Ann picked up Gussie and they raced back to Lubbock. Meanwhile, the suitcase that she had packed so carefully remained guarding the front door. Gussie had been so frantic that morning that she had forgotten the bag that was the reason she had gone home in the first place.

D'Ann drove fast. They traveled the seventy miles to Lubbock in less than an hour. By 6 A.M., they were back at Clyde's bedside. Gussie barely had time to kiss him before attendants came to take him to surgery. Gussie and D'Ann walked beside his gurney. The husband and wife—the newlyweds—held hands.

"I'm just worried about Gussie," Clyde told D'Ann. "This is hard on her. I didn't mean to do this to her."

When they reached two black doors—the color so ominous—Gussie and Clyde kissed again and parted.

"I can't help thinkin' about that white deer," he said.

"I'd shoot it for you," she said.

"Gussie, did you ever hunt anything in your life?"

"I went rabbit hunting with my daddy a couple of times, but I never hit anything."

"That's what I thought."

"I could learn."

"Thanks, Honey Bun."

Clyde entered the operating room, the OR, and Gussie retreated to the surgery waiting room with its uncomfortable seats. D'Ann waited with her.

Hours spent in hospital waiting rooms are the longest hours in the history of time. And of these hours, the longest are those spent in the surgery waiting room. The chairs grow more and more uncomfortable. The head aches. Eyes grow bloodshot and raw watching the waiting-room door, waiting for the surgeon to appear with good news or heartbreaking news. Doctor after doctor arrives, but they aren't your doctor. Family after family smiles or cries uncontrollably.

About noon, after an endless morning, Dr. Shoukfeh finally did make an appearance. He told Gussie that the operation had gone well, but there had been a complication. He had something that he wanted to show her. Would she please come with him?

The doctor escorted Gussie to a room equipped with a VCR and a TV. He played a videotape for her, one not so different from the movie *Innerspace,* about a tiny human voyaging through the pathways of the body. She saw a camera's view as it voyaged through her husband's veins and arteries. The camera kept running into sludge. Dr. Shoukfeh explained that these were blood clots. He said they should be cleaned out or Clyde might lose his left leg. Cleaning would mean more surgery. Gussie sagged. The years were piling on.

Then Dr. Shoukfeh took Gussie into the recovery room to see her husband. She found Clyde awake, telling the nurses that he was worried about Gussie. He was afraid he had become a burden. These were supposed to be their honeymoon days, weeks, months. Instead, they were hell.

Another doctor loomed over my dad. He was introduced as Dr. Burt Fowler. His specialty was cleaning out veins and arteries. He had a crewcut and a military bearing. When he talked, he seemed to be barking orders. With the comforting bedside manner of Dr. Strangelove, Dr. Fowler told my father that he needed a second operation, this one to clean out the blood clots. Clyde agreed to the surgery, gave his permission, even though he was out of his mind at the time. Later he had no recollection of this conversation.

Clyde was nuts, but he still remembered his mantra: "I'm worried about Gussie. This isn't fair . . ."

Once again, Gussie and D'Ann retreated to the waiting room. Hours spent in hospital waiting rooms are the longest hours in the history of time. And of these hours, the longest . . .

At around five in the afternoon, the long-awaited doctor appeared in the doorway of the surgery waiting room. He was smiling and almost jumping up and down. The marines had finally taken Iwo Jima, and he had helped raise the flag. He reported that the veins and arteries had been cleaned out and everything had gone even better than he had hoped. In all, Clyde had spent eleven hours in surgery—and Gussie the same eleven hours in the waiting room—but it all had a happy ending.

Much relieved, Gussie and D'Ann went out for a fast dinner at the Kettle restaurant, which was nearby. D'Ann's father, a banking legend in that part of Texas, joined them.

While they were dining, I arrived at St. Mary's Hospital, having just flown in from New York. As I entered his room, I reached down and tapped my father's toe to say hello.

"No!" yelled my dad. "That's my sore foot."

"I'm sorry."

I sat down, and he told me about his thoroughly exhausting day.

"But I'm okay," he said. "Who I'm worried about is Gussie. I didn't mean to get her into all this. I sure didn't."

For better, for worse, in sickness and in health. Would she stay? I wondered myself. I remembered what had happened to my wife's grandfather; when he got sick, his second wife simply decamped to Florida. She rarely came back, but she did manage to show up for the funeral years later. So I knew that people sometimes did leave. I didn't know Gussie well enough to be certain what she would do. But I did know my father well enough to know: If she left, it would break his heart, maybe even kill him. What would he have to live for?

"It's not fair to her," my dad said.

A nurse entered with a large and mysterious machine. It looked a little like an old-fashioned, bulky radio.

"I'm here to check your foot," the nurse explained. "We need to try to find a pulse."

She uncovered my father's foot—the left one, the one I had touched—and went to work with a stethoscope, which was plugged into the old radio. She listened just below his ankle.

"Be careful," Dad said. "That's sore."

She listened a little lower down, then a little higher up, then a little to the left, a little to the right, on the bottom of his foot, and on the top.

"Can you hear anything?" I asked.

"No, I'm afraid not," she said, taking the stethoscope out of her ears. "Sometimes I think I hear something, but then I think it's my imagination." She shrugged. "Do you want to listen?"

"Sure."

She handed me the stethoscope. I listened, but I didn't hear anything either. I remembered a similar scene back when Lesley was in labor with Taylor. The obstetrician had me listen to Taylor's heartbeat. Then he said: I think her heart is skipping beats, don't you? Once he put the thought into my head, that's what I heard: thump—THUMP THUMP—thump thump thump—THUMP. And I thought: If I'm being called in as a consultant, we're in trouble! That was when they rushed Lesley in for an emergency cesarean. But now I didn't hear any thumps at all. Once again, I was frightened.

That night I drove Gussie the seventy miles back to Spur to fetch her forgotten suitcase.

A belt of straw and ivy buds, with coral clasps and amber studs: And if these pleasures may you move . . .

34

The Last Full Measure of Devotion

Give me your arm, old toad;
Help me down Cemetery Road.
—Philip Larkin,
"Toads Revisited"

We slept at Clyde and Gussie's new home that night. The next morning, I got up early and went out to the cemetery. I wanted to visit not only my mother but my sister, Sharon. She was killed in a car crash on May 10, 1967. A couple of felonious drag racers hit her Dodge Dart broadside. The first officer on the scene broke the jaw of one of the racers. I generally disapprove of police brutality, but not always.

I drove into the graveyard and then bounced along a bumpy path until I saw the broad tombstone with LATHAM carved on it. Beneath our family name were three given names: Sharon, Launa, Clyde. He already had his name carved on his tombstone. Clyde and Gussie had agreed that he would be buried beside his first wife, Launa, and she would eventually lie next to her late husband Bill.

Now I noticed the dead flowers on my mother's grave, and these dry blooms set in motion a train of memories. I remembered my uncle Joe Latham telling his "son" Tommy: "Go out to the cemetery and take all the flowers off your mother's grave." That was the day Lee Latham was buried, and she was covered in flowers. Tommy asked: "Why?" Joe said: "I'm gonna want to go out to visit your mother's grave, and I don't want to find dead flowers on it." I could see her headstone from where I sat. There weren't any flowers, alive or dead. Joe didn't visit his wife's grave anymore because he now lay beside her. There weren't any flowers on his grave either. Tommy would always make sure of that.

*T*ommy actually had two fathers, one dead and buried, the other still alive. Joe was the putative dad, but his brother Abo was the real father. Anyway, that is what a lot of people in Spur believed. They believed it because of gossip spread by good old Pop Latham—my grandfather, Clyde's father, Joe's father, and Abo's father. One of Pop's son's made love to a woman who just happened to be married to another one of Pop's son's. The result: Tommy. Maybe Pop was just a mean old man spreading false tales . . .

From birth, Tommy found himself in the middle of an emotional tug-of-war. Both Joe and Abo courted him. Each seemed to be trying to prove to Tommy—and to the world—that he was the real father. And the whole town watched.

Joe's other children, four of them, grew up and left Spur for towns and cities where there were more opportunities. Tommy tried to leave. For a while, he moved out to Tucson, where there were lots of well-paying jobs. But he didn't stick. He was irresistibly drawn back to Spur, drawn back to the tug-of-war, drawn back to the place where two fathers wanted him.

In 1991, Joe was dying in a Lubbock hospital, but he desperately wanted to die at home. Tommy, the good son, broke him out of St. Mary's and headed for Spur. Joe kept telling him to drive faster, faster, faster because he was afraid he wouldn't live to see his home again. Tommy kept pressing harder on the accelerator. When they reached home—after covering seventy miles in forty minutes— Tommy carried his father into the house. The son laid his dad down on the couch. Joe took a last breath and died in Tommy's arms. But they had won the race. After the funeral, Tommy went out to the cemetery and took all the flowers off his father's grave.

Then Tommy moved into Joe's house. Abo moved, too. He rented the house next door to Tommy's.

*S*tanding there, looking at the dirt that covered Mom, I recalled once again her terrible last days, sixty-nine of them in the hospital. I remembered how my father had endangered his own health by staying with her around the clock. Of course, I was there, too, most of the time, but he was there all the time.

"How you makin' out?" I would ask over and over again.

"Don't worry about me," my father would say. "Save your worry for your mama."

"Can you walk?"

"Not much, but I don't have to. I'm just gonna sit right here."

He was exhausted, seemingly shell-shocked, but he wouldn't leave. Remembering that terrible time, I recalled a phrase that Lincoln had used in another cemetery: "the last full measure of devotion." In those sixty-nine days, my father had paid Lincoln's high price.

The phrase kept repeating itself in my mind. The last full measure of devotion. The words fit my father's devotion even better than they did those boys who died at Gettysburg. Who knew why they fought and fell that day? Because they were afraid of being considered cowards? Or they just didn't know how to stop what they had started? But my father's long hours of constant physical and emotional pain really had been devotion. He had given all he could for as long as she was alive to accept it. He had done *all* he could. He had proved his love, his devotion, completely. He had nothing left to prove to me, to himself, to anyone. Nothing that happened later, not his remarriage, not his new life, would or could diminish what he had done.

I was beginning to accept that my father had earned the right to move on.

A belt of straw and ivy buds, with coral clasps and amber studs: and if these pleasures may you move, come live with me . . .

35
$\mathscr{O}$uch!

Out, damned spot!
—Shakespeare,
Macbeth

A small black dot appeared on my father's left heel. It was a black cloud that grew larger and larger. The skin there wasn't getting enough blood and was dying. Long hospital days and long hospital nights. Then longer days and longer nights. Being exhausted from doing nothing all day and all night. Gussie was worried about Clyde, he was worried about her, and I was worried about them both. Would he get well? Would she break his heart? I didn't know. But every time she left the room, she gave him a kiss—on the mouth, a real I-mean-business kiss. Still?

Gussie and I ate dinner every evening at the Black-Eyed Pea restaurant on Slide Road facing the South Plains Mall. The vegetables were so good that's all we ate. Fried okra, broccoli casserole, fried corn on the cob, red beans and rice, mashed baked potatoes, and of course black-eyed peas. These vegetarian dinners reminded Gussie of her days as an orphan, when the meat dishes almost never made it to the orphans' table. But now she passed up meat willingly. Times change.

My new stepmother and I stayed in adjoining rooms at the Country Inn, which is three blocks from the hospital, forty dollars a night. The motel made most of its money selling rooms to people who had critically ill loved ones. St. Mary's served a wide expanse of West Texas and even parts of New Mexico. Lots of folks lived too far away to commute. The hospital's parking lot was always crowded with RV's where whole families lived while one of theirs was getting better or getting worse or dying. Day and night, helicopter ambulances could be heard bringing in patients from faraway farms, ranches, and small towns.

Gussie and I took turns sitting beside my father's hospital bed watching that black spot grow larger. Lots of visitors trooped through that room. They were from Spur, and they had driven seventy miles—one hundred and forty round-trip—to see my dad. Several of them he'd known in first grade. Others he'd known before first grade. Some were long-ago football players my dad had coached. The visitors ranged in age from ninety down to toddlers. I kept remembering what Lyndon Johnson's father, Sam, used to say about small Texas towns: They know when you're sick and care when you die.

It was like a ritual: Every visitor who entered the room reached over and tapped my father's left foot. It was elevated on a pillow, and the big toe raised the sheet like the center pole of a circus tent. Old friends, new friends, just casual acquaintances, they all touched that very sore toe.

"No!" my dad would say, but always too late. "That's my sore foot."

Then on their way out, they would reach out and touch that foot again. They just couldn't resist.

"Ouch!"

"Oh, sorry."

The Pitchfork's Moorhouse family came often. Clyde was especially glad to see them, these latter-day knights and damsels of the range. They had driven even farther than the others. When they walked through the door, Bob Moorhouse, the eternal cowboy, would always toss his cowboy hat on my dad's upturned toe.

"Ouch!"

After several days, the black spot on Clyde's heel stopped growing. The doctors said he could go home. I went home, too.

A belt of straw and ivy buds, with coral clasps and amber studs: and if these pleasures may you move, come live with me, and be my love.

36
$\mathcal{H}$ell

Lord Chief Justice to Falstaff: Have you not a moist eye, a dry hand, a yellow cheek, a white beard, a decreasing leg? . . .

—Shakespeare, *Henry IV, Part 2*

I got a disturbing call from Gussie. She told me that my father was in the Spur nursing home. I felt sick. I knew how much he hated—and feared—that home. He had gone in it once, to visit his hundred-year-old Aunt Ol, but he got so upset he never went back. He couldn't stand the sight of all those pathetic human wrecks. He had even talked me out of going to see Aunt Ol. He said it would just depress me, and she wouldn't remember anyway. As far as he was concerned, the nursing home had been de-signed by Dante. It was the last place on earth he would have wanted to go. Gussie said she had no choice.

"I was exhausted, just totally exhausted," she told me on the phone. "I didn't even have time to wash my clothes. He needs around-the-clock care. I simply can't do that. You've got to understand."

"I do," I said, but I didn't.

I couldn't believe that she had consigned my father to hell. Now I could see how right my father had been to worry about Gussie. She couldn't take it. She was probably packing right now. Of course, I shouldn't really blame her: She had looked forward to a very different sort of honeymoon. No, I shouldn't blame her at all, but I did.

"Gussie, we'll pay for round-the-clock care," I said. "At home."

"No," she said. "The nursing home's the right place for him. He wants to stay there."

I didn't believe her, although I didn't say as much. She was crying.

*T*hen I got a call from Dr. Chandler. He told me that my dad was back in the hospital. It almost sounded like good news: He was out of that damned nursing home. But of course the news wasn't all good. The doctor told me that if the circulation in his left leg didn't improve—

"We might have to take off his leg."

I headed for the airport once again.

The shepherd swains shall dance and sing . . .

$\mathcal{T}$he Wounded Surgeon

My most kyndly nurse.
—Edmund Spenser,
"Prothalamion"

Dr. Fowler said we would wait four more days. Then if there was no improvement, the time would have come to get in touch with an orthopedic surgeon. That would mean amputation. Clyde would be a cripple. And what would Gussie do? I could tell that my father was worried, and I was, too.

The doctors and nurses kept coming in, checking my father's left foot. They still couldn't find a pulse. And he was in great pain. He kept taking pain killers and spending much of his time passed out. When he wasn't unconscious, he wished he were. He slept as much as a male lion (who sleeps twenty hours a day). And he would have slept more if he could.

Now when well-meaning visitors touched his foot, Clyde simply couldn't stand it. Hearing footsteps in the corridor, he would start his mantra: "Don't touch my foot, don't touch my foot, don't touch my foot . . ." I would tackle anybody who didn't get the message.

My father wanted a towel placed under his left heel; then he would ask to have it taken away. He wanted the foot of the bed raised; then he wanted it lowered. Nothing was comfortable.

The first day passed with no improvement.

The doctors were attempting to treat the circulatory failure by dripping blood thinners into his arm day and night. He also got ultrasound treatments that were supposed to help break up blood clots.

The second day, we thought the black spot looked a little better. It seemed to be turning brown. Hooray! Gussie gave Clyde a solid kiss, and then she and I went out to celebrate at the Black-Eyed Pea. Fried corn. Fried okra. The whole drill plus a glass of terrible red wine from a local West Texas vineyard.

When we got back to the hospital, we checked the dead spot again. We couldn't be certain. It looked black. Where had the brown gone? Maybe it had just been the light. Or maybe the light was wrong now.

Gussie and Clyde held hands.

The third day, the spot kept changing color. And size! Or else the changes were in the eyes of the beholders. Our hopes went down, then up, then down again. But my father kept hurting. That never changed. Gussie held his hand. He apologized for putting her through this ordeal.

The fourth day, the spot was definitely brown. It was brown every time we looked at it. It didn't change. We were relieved. Clyde and Gussie held hands.

Around noon, a young nurse's aide entered looking extremely nervous. She was actually shaking.

"I'm here to g-g-give you your b-b-bath," she said.

"Did you ever do this before?" asked Clyde.

"No."

"Do you know what to do?"

"No."

"Do you want me to tell you?"

"Would you?" She smiled. "I'd really appreciate it. You're a lifesaver."

Clyde told her where to wash and how to do it. He warned her not to touch his sore foot. He couldn't stand it. She washed him carefully and thoroughly all over—except for his left foot and his genitals.

"Am I supposed to w-w-wash th-that too?" she asked anxiously.

"The other nurses do."

"Okay, here g-g-goes."

As the nurse's aide reached for Clyde's penis, Gussie's eyes got very large. The young woman's fingers trembled, which made them tickle.

"You need to wash under the foreskin," said my uncircumcised father. "That's where all the germs get hung up."

Gussie's eyes got even bigger as the young nurse got down to business. She pushed back the foreskin and scrubbed. She did good work. When she finished, she looked up and smiled. Even under these rather trying circumstances, Clyde had managed to charm her.

"Thank you very much for helping me," she said. "I learned a lot."

At around 6:00 in the evening, Dr. Fowler came in accompanied by another physician. He introduced Dr. Guy Fogel, an orthopedic surgeon. We were not happy to see him. Excited, defensive, we told the doctors that the black spot had turned brown.

"That spot doesn't have much to do with it," said Dr. Fowler in his parade-ground voice.

"Can you straighten out your knee?" asked Dr. Fogel.

My father tried.

"No," he said.

"We're going to have to amputate," said Dr. Fowler.

Gussie and I were very upset. Clyde took the news matter-of-factly.

"Anyway, maybe it won't hurt anymore," he said.

"I'm an amputee myself," said Dr. Fogel. "The same leg as you. Amputated at the knee, just like you will be. And I'm getting around all right."

"How long until I can play golf?" asked Clyde.

"About six months," said Dr. Fogel.

The shepherd swains shall dance and sing for your delight each May morning . . .

38

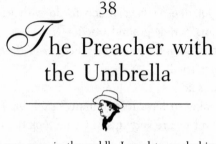

$\mathscr{T}$he Preacher with
the Umbrella

It was once in the saddle I used to go dashing.
—"The Streets of Laredo"

Early in the morning, Gussie kissed Clyde good-bye.

"Are you thinking about your white deer?" she asked.

"How'd you know?"

"Just keep on thinking about him. Maybe that'll help."

"Maybe. You be good now. I mean it. I hear lots of ro-
mances start in hospital waitin' rooms."

They laughed, and he went through the black doors. It
was May 1st, the first day of the best month of the
year.

Soon the people from Spur started to arrive. They found
Gussie and me in the surgery waiting room. They had
heard and had come to circle round us. There was Stacy
Campbell, the wife of the mortician. But actually she was
more than that. She took an active part in the business
and was really co-mortician. By now, she and Gussie both

loved each other. There was Dixie Robertson, the wife of the druggist Dan, who had four children whose names all began with D: Derek, Dawn, Danielle, and Dione. This alliterative family used to lend us its sailboat to glide around White River Lake. Dixie had been sick and over-weight for years, but now she was trim and healthy. There was also Scrub Hawley the bicycle enthusiast, who had actually raced in the Tour de France a few years ago. He is short, muscular, a human fireplug, but a fireplug without an ounce of fat. And of course D'Ann Pierce, who owned the ranch where Clyde and Gussie lived.

Naturally, Brother Larry Burton, the new Methodist preacher, was there too. The old preacher, my father's friend, had been "run off" because of alleged sexual pec-cadillos, which I doubted. The preacher before him had been "run off" too, because his wife used pay telephones a lot. And who could she be calling on such a phone but her lover? Otherwise, why didn't she call from home or the church? The bad thing about small towns was that every-body snooped and gossiped. The good thing was that ev-eryone showed up on the day your father had his left leg cut off at the knee. Brother Larry, the new man, is sandy-haired, pot-bellied, kindhearted. He always carries an um-brella to prove he is praying for rain and believes in an-swered prayers. We all sat in a row at the back of the waiting room.

Sitting there, I tried to write. I was working on a screen-play and had brought a laptop computer to the waiting room. I concentrated so hard on the writing—in order to shut out thoughts of the operation—that I actually made pretty good progress. Gussie talked to the people from

Spur the whole time. I don't think she breathed. Each to his or her own blocking mechanism.

After a little over two hours, Dr. Shoukfeh, my father's heart doctor, appeared in the doorway. He told Gussie and me that he wanted to talk to us in private. Then he led the way to a small room where a lot of bad news had been passed on over the years. Why was he the one who had come to talk to us? Why not the one-legged orthopedic surgeon? Something must have happened to my father's heart during the operation. My stepmother and I were terrified. We didn't dare look at the doctor—or even each other.

"His heart came through the surgery fine," said Dr. Shoukfeh. "He's strong. The operation went very well."

Gussie and I both laughed out loud.

The shepherd swains shall dance and sing for your delight each May morning: If these delights your mind may move . . .

$\mathscr{A}$ Setback

Pain penetrates

Me drop
by drop
—Mary Barnard,
    translating Sappho

They wheeled my one-legged father into a room with a view of a lake. He was still asleep from the anesthesia. Stacy Campbell, the undertaker, was crying softly. Gussie and D'Ann hugged each other. I couldn't keep from staring at my father's stump under the sheet. I found myself trying to imagine where his left foot was now. Then I tried not to imagine it, to put it out of my mind, but I couldn't. Did they just throw it in the garbage? I didn't want to know, but I couldn't help wondering.

The telephone started ringing. People from all over wanted to know how the operation had gone. Lesley called from New York. Nola called from California. Of course, there were lots of calls from Spur. Gussie and I took turns answering the phone. We told everybody that the operation had gone very well and Clyde was going to be fine.

But we were wrong.

*M*y father woke up with a terrible pain not only in his leg—his stump—but also in his stomach. Were they somehow connected, his leg and his gut? Were they wired into the same switchboard? Was there a short in the circuit?

My dad could control his suffering to a certain extent by pushing a button on a pump that dripped pain killers into his arm. Relief on demand. Some relief anyway.

Gussie and I stayed with him twenty-four hours a day for three days. We slept on roll-away cots provided by the hospital.

"My foot hurts," Clyde said.

"Do you want me to rub it?" asked Gussie.

"Not that foot. The one that isn't there anymore. It just burns right on the bottom of my foot."

When Dr. Fogel, the one-legged surgeon, came by to check on his patient, Clyde asked: "How long do these phantom pains go on?"

The doctor said: "That's hard to say. My missing foot still hurts me every day."

"Oh."

As the blur of days and nights passed, the pain from the cutting and sawing got better. The phantom pains remained about the same. But the pain in his stomach got worse. Something was clearly wrong, and we were all very worried.

"I'm so sorry, Gussie," Clyde said. "I wouldn't have done this to you for the world."

The shepherd swains shall dance and sing for your delight each May morning: If these delights your mind may move, then live with me . . .

40

he Swat Team

She left the web, she left the loom,
She made three paces thro' the room,
She saw the water lily bloom,
She saw the helmet and the plume,
    She looked down on Camelot.
Out flew the web and floated wide;
The mirror cracked from side to side.
"The curse has come upon me," cried
    The Lady of Shalott.
          —Alfred, Lord Tennyson,
          "The Lady of Shalott"

My father lost his appetite completely. I kept telling him
to eat, but he wouldn't. Or rather he just couldn't. Still he
never lost his charm. When a nurse would appear to check
on him, he would say:

"I'd tell you how good this food is, but it's not polite to
talk with your mouth full."

The nurse would laugh and leave.

I would ask: "If it's so good, why aren't you eating it?"

He would say: "You gotta try to make people feel good if you can." .

But his abdomen kept hurting. Worse and worse.

A young woman in a white coat glided into the room. Her name was Dr. Melinda Beth Nickels, and she belonged to a group of surgeons who called themselves the SWAT team. They handled most of the triage cases in and around Lubbock. Plane crashes and train wrecks, automobile accidents and lightning burns, knifings and shootings—they were all their meat. If you needed some cutting done *right now,* then you needed them. Surgery has long been a male bastion, and what was true of this line of work in general was even more true of the macho SWAT team. Moreover, this was not just anywhere, this was Texas. And not just Texas but West Texas, the last refuge of that larger-than-life male icon: the cowboy. But now the SWAT team had finally taken on a woman. She radiated the kind of calm you needed at such overwhelming catastrophes as a crash site or a major bombing—or your father's life-and-death struggle.

Dr. Nickels rushed my father right back into the operating room. Once again Gussie and I spent long hours in the surgery waiting room. Once again Spur showed up to sit with us through this ordeal. Of course, repetition—practice—did not make these waits any easier. How much trauma could my father's body take? And how much could Gussie take? So far she had had plenty of "in sickness" and hardly any "in health" at all. My seat hurt, my head hurt, my eyes hurt, my brain hurt. I was sure hers did too. We kept our eye on the door.

Worried, pessimistic, I found myself reviewing genera-
tions of grief. The West had cost my great-grandmother
two husbands and two sons. Gussie had lost her first husband after only three years of marriage. Gussie's daughter,
Nola, lost her first husband in a plane crash. I lost my
sister in a car wreck. I wondered: Do some families have
death-by-violence imprinted on their genes? And now my
father's new beginning, his new love, his new life, seemed
to be turning tragic.

When Dr. Nickels finally appeared in the doorway of
the waiting room, I tried to rush to her, but I was so stiff I
could hardly move. Gussie got to her first with me not too
far behind.

Dr. Nickels said the surgery had gone well. When she
opened Clyde up, she found that his intestines had literally tied themselves in a knot. They were completely
blocked. She had cut out the knot.

*T*hat night in the intensive care unit, Clyde lay dying.
Doctors and nurses were running all over the ICU grab-
bing IV bottles and syringes. They rolled in a machine that
looked like it belonged on the space shuttle and attached
it to him. Then a sleepy Dr. Nickels arrived on the run at
3 A.M. She barked orders. My father fought back. The crisis passed. Gussie and I were both wrecks.

Shortly before noon, Dr. Nickels dropped in to check
on Clyde.

"Well, I'm still alive and kickin'," he said. "They tell me
that's your fault."

"I can't take all the blame," she said. "A lot of folks
around here helped out."

"So there's enough blame to go around?"

"That's right."

*T*he next day, while my father's condition was still considered grave, Lesley and Taylor arrived. They visited Clyde in ICU. Lesley squeezed his hand. We all crowded around the bed.

Gussie sat there exhausted, worn down, worn out, but still trying to put on a bright face with the aid of makeup. I could see the pain behind her vague eyes, along her brittle limbs, in the knots of her arthritic hands.

"How are you?" Lesley asked her.

"Oh, I'll be all right," Gussie said. "Don't worry about me."

I remembered my father saying something similar when my mother was in the hospital for so long. . . . Don't worry about him. . . . Now it was don't worry about her. . . . I slowly began to realize that Gussie was doing for Clyde what he had done for my mother. She was exhausting herself for him. She was enduring physical pain for him. She was even endangering her own health in an attempt to do all she could to heal him. She was offering her own last true measure of devotion—only I certainly hoped it wouldn't be the last. I hoped they would be able to offer each other devotion for years and years to come.

I leaned over and hugged Gussie. Perhaps I hugged her a little too tightly. Her old eyes bulged slightly. Then Gussie, being an easy crier, started shedding tears. I cried, too, cried for my mother, who was now finally dead. But I cried for more also. I cried because I was feeling the happiness that comes out of the sharpest pain.

"I'm worried about Gussie," the patient whispered to my wife. "Maybe she should just go back to California. What do you think?"

"Gussie isn't going anywhere," said Lesley.

"How do you know?"

"Because she's in love."

The shepherd swains shall dance and sing for your delight each May morning: If these delights your mind may move, then live with me and be my love.

$\mathscr{E}$pilogue

Omnia vincit amor: et nos cedamus amori.
—Virgil, *Ecologues*

My father wasn't going anywhere either and for the same reason. He wasn't about to depart this earth because he was—is—in love with Gussie. He wanted to go home with her and live his life with her. He was as sick as anybody could be, and yet he battled his way back. If he hadn't been in love, he would have gone quietly to lie down next to my mother and my sister.

When his several cuts were healing well, Clyde was transferred to the rehabilitation wing of the hospital. A leg-maker came and measured him, and after a few days returned with the new leg.

Later, when I called Gussie in Spur to tell her the good news, I described the new leg: It looked surprisingly like a golf tee with a cup on top and a thin shank. The cup was white plastic, the shank steel. I went on to tell her about helping a couple of brawny male nurses lift Clyde up and set him on his feet. Then holding onto parallel bars, he walked half a dozen steps.

When we got back to his room, Clyde called Gussie. He almost shouted: "Gussie, I can walk!"

So who was the better writer, my father the football coach or his son the author? He had summed up the miracle in three words.

A few days later, Clyde was well enough to ride on his own float in the old-timers' day parade. This float celebrated the fiftieth anniversary of one of his teams, and a half dozen of his football players rode with him. For the occasion, he wore his wedding present—the big black cowboy hat—and a big smile. A huge sign, popping and crackling in the wind, proclaimed in block letters:

HONORING CLYDE LATHAM

The float was followed by a posse of cowboys on horseback.

That was a year ago, a year of changes in Spur. The old movie theater, the Palace, has been refurbished and is about to reopen. The brave new owner, Spur's newest movie mogul, is a spry ninety-year-old woman. There is a spark of life in this old town—and the old people in it— yet. Just when you think everything is over, when life seems to have come and gone, the movie starts again.

Clyde is still doing fine. In the old days, when I called him, he would tell me what he had shot on the golf course that day. He was always enthusiastic. Now when I call him, every day right after dinner, he tells me how far he walked that day.

"Across the living room . . . across the living room and back again . . . up and down the ramp at the back door . . . into church . . . into the drugstore for morning coffee with the guys . . . to the first tee . . . hit a few balls . . . cooked dinner for Gussie . . ."

He is more excited about these achievements than he ever was about a golf score. His enthusiasm, its sound in his voice, is the same, but amplified, intensified. He is living his life. To paraphrase Virgil, there's nothing love can't throw and hogtie.

Not long ago, I flew down to West Texas for another of my father's birthdays. I landed in Lubbock and rented a car. Then I drove those long miles through the flat cotton fields. When I finally reached my destination, I entered through the back door and looked around. They weren't in the kitchen. They weren't in the living room.

I found them in their den, sitting side by side in their recliners, fast asleep, smiling, holding hands. It was a pretty old world.

Come live with me and be my love, and we will all the pleasures prove that valleys, groves, hills, and fields, woods, or steepy mountain yields.

And we will sit upon the rocks, seeing the shepherds feed their flocks, by shallow rivers to whose falls melodious birds sing madrigals.

And I will make you beds of roses and a thousand fragrant posies, a cap of flowers, and a kirtle embroidered all with leaves of myrtle;

A gown made of the finest wool which from our pretty lambs we pull; fair lined slippers for the cold, with buckles of the purest gold;

A belt of straw and ivy buds, with coral clasps and amber studs: And if these pleasures may you move, come live with me, and be my love.

The shepherd swains shall dance and sing for your delight each May morning: If these delights your mind may move, then live with me and be my love.

ABOUT THE AUTHOR

AARON LATHAM is best known for his novels and screenplays, including *Urban Cowboy*. He has been a regular contributor to publications such as *Esquire, Rolling Stone, The New York Times,* and *New York* magazine.